English Unlimited

B1

Pre-intermediate A
Coursebook

Alex Tilbury, Theresa Clementson, Leslie Anne Hendra & David Rea
Course consultant: Adrian Doff

CAMBRIDGE
UNIVERSITY PRESS

CAMBRIDGE
UNIVERSITY PRESS

University Printing House, Cambridge CB2 8BS, United Kingdom

One Liberty Plaza, 20th Floor, New York, NY 10006, USA

477 Williamstown Road, Port Melbourne, VIC 3207, Australia

4843/24, 2nd Floor, Ansari Road, Daryaganj, Delhi – 110002, India

79 Anson Road, #06–04/06, Singapore 079906

Torre de los Parques, Colonia Tlacoquemécatl del Valle, Mexico City CP 03200, Mexico

Cambridge University Press is part of the University of Cambridge.

It furthers the University's mission by disseminating knowledge in the pursuit of education, learning and research at the highest international levels of excellence.

www.cambridge.org
Information on this title: www.cambridge.org/9781107621510

English Unlimited Split Combo Edition © Cambridge University Press 2013
Adapted from English Unlimited © Cambridge University Press 2010

English Unlimited Split Combo Edition first published 2013
Reprinted 2016

Printed in Italy by Rotolito Lombarda S.p.A.

A catalogue record for this publication is available from the British Library

ISBN 978-1-107-62151-0 Pre-intermediate A Coursebook with e-Portfolio and
                          Self-study Pack (Workbook with DVD-ROM)
ISBN 978-1-107-65453-2 Pre-intermediate Teacher's Pack
ISBN 978-0-521-69779-8 Pre-intermediate Class Audio CDs

How to use this coursebook

Every unit of this book is divided into sections, with clear, practical **goals** for learning. The 'R' pages to which students are directed comprise sections of activities and reference material that follow after the units.

The first four pages of the unit help you build your language skills and knowledge. These pages include speaking, listening, reading, writing, grammar, vocabulary and pronunciation activities. They are followed by a **Target activity** which will help you put together what you have learned.

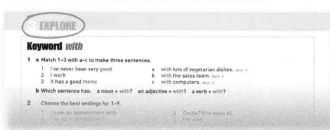

The **Explore** section of the unit begins with a **Keyword**, which looks at one of the most common and useful words in English. It also includes either an **Across cultures** or an **Independent learning** section, and then an **Explore speaking** or **Explore writing** task. The Explore section gives you extra language and skills work, all aiming to help you become a better communicator in English and a more effective learner.

The **Look again** section takes another look at the target language for the unit, helping you to review and extend your learning.
Sometimes you will also find this recycling symbol with the goals, to show when a particular goal is not new but is recycling language that you have met before.

This symbol shows you when you can hear and practise the correct pronunciation of key language, using the audio DVD-ROM.

The **e-Portfolio** DVD-ROM contains useful reference material for all the units, as well as self-assessment to help you test your own learning, and Wordcards to help you test your vocabulary learning.

You can do more practice by yourself using the **Self-study Pack**, which includes a workbook and interactive DVD-ROM.

The DVD-ROM contains video and over 300 interactive activities.

Contents

Contents

Acknowledgements

The authors would like to thank all the team at CUP for their ideas, support and commitment to *English Unlimited*, in particular their editors Karen Momber, Greg Sibley and Keith Sands, and David Lawton for his work on the cover and page design. They'd also like to thank Adrian Doff for his consistently encouraging and remarkably detailed feedback; and Dave Willis, Jane Willis, Alison Sharpe and Sue Ullstein for their ideas and inspiration in the early days of this project.

Thanks are also due to Michael Stuart Clark, Dariusz Klimkowicz, Monica Koorichh and Li Mills for particular ideas and contributions.

Alex Tilbury would like to dedicate his work on *English Unlimited* to Geoffrey William Tilbury, Carol Tilbury and Sławek Smolorz, with love and thanks.

David Rea would like to thank the students, teachers, trainers and staff at IH Kraków, IH Heliopolis, IH Buenos Aires, IH Paris and IH London for all the support, development and fun over the years. He'd also like to thank Emma McLachlan: the most beautiful woman in the world.

Leslie Anne Hendra would like to thank her four long-time students and friends in Japan: Junko Terajima, Eiko Kanai, Akiko Tsuzuki and Akiko Ohno. With much appreciation for all the wonderful time we spent together.

Theresa Clementson would like to thank Anthony, Sam and Megan for their ideas, support and unwavering confidence, and Cristina Rimini for her help and advice on all matters TEFL over the years.

The authors and publishers would like to thank the following teachers for invaluable feedback they provided when reviewing draft material:

Howard Smith, Merryn Grimley (UK); María de los Ángeles Vélez Guzmán (Mexico); Justyna Kubica (Poland); Gill Hamilton (Spain); Martin Goosey (Korea); Catherine Land (Czech Republic); Iris Grallert, Donna Liersch (Germany); Rachel Connabeer (Italy); Jamelea Nader (Japan); Amanda Gamble (Turkey); and the various members of the Cambridge Adult Panel.

The authors and publishers are also grateful to the following contributors:

Design and page make-up: Stephanie White at Kamae Design

Picture research: Hilary Luckcock

Photography: Gareth Boden

Audio recordings: John Green at Audio Workshop and id-Audio, London

The authors and publishers would like to thank all of those who took part in the authentic recording sessions, especially:

Annie Gentil, Alba Higgins, David Warwick, Susanne Neubert, Siew Wan Chai, Xi Yen Tan, Paula Porroni, Natalie Krol, Leonardo Solano, Megan Rivers-Moore, Manuel Arroyo-Kalin, Pham Thi Thanh An, Andrew Reid, Richa Bansal, Masha Sutton, Seung Yang, Tom Boyd, Fran Disken, Astrid Gonzales-Rabade, Anri Iwasaki, Annie Gentil, Martin Huarte-Espinosa, Ivan Gladstone, Nuria Gonzales-Rabade.

The authors and publishers acknowledge the following sources of copyright material and are grateful for the permissions granted. While every effort has been made, it has not always been possible to identify the sources of all the material used, or to trace all copyright holders. If any omissions are brought to our notice, we will be happy to include the appropriate acknowledgements on reprinting.

With thanks to the WOMADelaide Foundation and writer David Sly for the extract on p11; Ruben Gonzalez, www.OlympicMotivation.com, for the text on p13; Judi Bevan for the text on p27; Melissa Plaut for the text on p36 taken from: http://newyorkhack.blogspot.com/2006/08/cow-catcher.html. Reproduced by permission of Melissa Plaut; Microcredit Summit Campaign for the extracts on p45, Pre-intermediate A R-3. Reproduced by permission of Microcredit Summit Campaign; Mark Glaser for the text on p110 taken from: http://www.pbs.org/mediashift/2006/03/open-source-reportingliving-your-life-online086.html. Copyright PBS 2006; Content copyright © Dr.Nandita Iyer for the text on p116; *The Metro* for the article 'The Cycle Washer' by Sarah Hills Pre-intermediate A R-3, © *The Metro*.

The publisher has used its best endeavours to ensure that the URLs for external websites referred to in this book are correct and active at the time of going to press. However, the publisher has no responsibility for the websites and can make no guarantee that a site will remain live or that the content is or will remain appropriate.

The publishers are grateful to the following for permission to reproduce copyright photographs and material:

Key: l = left, c = centre, r = right, t = top, b = bottom

Alamy Images/John Sylvester for p7(tc), /©JupiterImages/Comstock for p7(tl), /©Blend Images for p7(bl), /©OJO Images Ltd for p7(tr), /© OJO Images Ltd for p8(tl), /©Photo Resource Hawaii for p12(bl), /©Studio9 for p14(tr), /©Radius Images for p18(tl), /©Radius Images for p18(tc), /©Alex Segre for p18(bl), /©Jenny Matthews for p18(br), /©Radius Images for p20(t), /©Radius Images for p20(b), /©Dave Penman for p26(l), /©Peter Horree for p26(c), /©Matt Griggs for p26(r), /©Graham Corney for p27(l), /©Itani Images for p27(ltc), /©Mira for p27(lbc), /©Blend Images for p31(c), /©Steve Teague for p32(H), /©LOOK Die Bildagentur der Fotografen GmbH for p35, /© LOOK Die Bildagentur der Fotografen GmbH for p40(c), /©JTB Photo for p46(tr), /©imagebroker for p48(t), /©A T Willett for p52(t background), /©imagebroker for p52(tr), /©uli nusko for p52(tcr), /©Robert Read for p52(tc), /©Richard Naude for p56(tr), /©Rupert Horrox/Sylvia Cordaiy Photos Ltd for p71, /©Pictures Colour Library for p63, /©Andre Jenny for p64(t), /©Mark Dyball for p67(b), /©INTERFOTO Pressebildagentur for p69(t), /©INSADCO Photography for p70(B), /©40260.com for p70(bl), /©Image State for p74(A), /©Gary Cook for p79(t), /©Sunday Photo Europe a.s. for p79(b), /©Jeff Greenberg for p80, /©Ian Shaw for p81, /©View Stock for p82(b), /©Iain Masterston for p84(t), /©RedCopsticks.com LLC for p84(b), /©Roussel Bernard for p85(t), /©UpperCut Images for p87(tr), /©David Young-Wolff for p87(b), /©Guillen Photography for p95, /©Ashley Cooper for p99(b), /©croftsphoto for p102(tl), /©Blend Images for p106(bl), /©Elmtree Images for p118(l), /©Roy Lawe for p118(c), /©Hornbil Images for p118(r), /©Image Source Black for p119(bl), /©Digital Vision for p120, /©imagebroker for Pre-intermediate A R-5(cheese), /©Andrew Twort for Pre-intermediate A R-5(cream), /©foodfolio for Pre-intermediate A R-5(salad), /©Jeffrey Blackler for Pre-intermediate A R-5(sauces), /©Andre Jenny for Pre-intermediate A R-5(spices), /©mediablitzimages (UK) Ltd for Pre-intermediate A R-5(vegetables), /©B & Y Photography for Pre-intermediate A R-5(spaghetti), /©foodfolio for Pre-intermediate A R-5(bake), /©Edd Westmacott for Pre-intermediate A R-5(boil), /©Red Fred for Pre-intermediate A R-5(fry), /©foodfolio for Pre-intermediate A R-5(roast); Alex Gadsden for p50(r); Beinbecke Rare Book & Manuscript Library, Yale University for p68(l); Bob Lestina for p45; Bopha Devi, Docklands, Australia for p28(tc); Corbis/©Dan Forer/Beateworks for p7(br), /©LWA-Dann Tardif for p8(tr), /©Jim Craigmyle for p8(b), /©Studio Eye for p30(c), /©Bjoern Sigurdsoen/epa for p44, /©Jonny le Fortune/zefa for p46(tl), /©image 100 for p47, /©The Irish Image Collection for p56(tl), /©Corbis Premium RF for p74(C), /©Corbis Super RF for p74(D), /©Paul Almasy for p92(l), /©Peter Turnley for p102(tr), /©Bettmann for p103(b), /©Studio Eye for Pre-intermediate A R-5(grill); DK Images for Pre-intermediate A R-5(stir), /©Howard Shooter for p32G, /©Dave King for Pre-intermediate A R-5(shake); Egyptian Museum, Cairo for pp68(r), 73; Emporis GmbH for p90(tr); Fondation Le Corbusier for pp 92 (cl, cr, r); Getty Images/©Stone for p10(tcl), /©Altrendo Images for p10(tr), /©Image Bank for p18(bc), /©Gulf Images for p21, /©Photolibrary for p24(r), /©imagewerks for p46(bl), /©Timothy A Clary/AFP for p50(l), /©Harald Sund for p60(b), /©Paul Quayle for p66(tl), /©PNC for p66(tr), /©Alan Becker for p66(br), /©Stephen Hoeck for p70(bcr), /©Narinder Nanu/AFP for p93, /©Aurora for p100(l), /©Denis Poroy/AFP for p100(r), /©Steve Smith for p115, /©Mike Powell for p114(t); istockphoto/©Arkady Chubykin for p52(br), /©Mummu Media for p74(E); Dr Nandita Iyer for p116; PA Photos/AP Photo/Diane Bondareff for p36(l); Panos/©Tim A Hetherington for p64(b); Photolibrary/©OJO Images Ltd for p18(tr), /©Hans-Peter Merten for p28(tl), /©PhotoDisc for p31(t), /©Robert Lawson for p32(E), /©PhotoDisc for p66(bl), /©image100 for p74(B), /©Jon Arnold RF for p82(t), /©OJO Images for p83, /©Richard Glover for p90(tl), /©Warwick Kent for p90(b), /©Juan Carlos Munoz for p104, /©Robert Harding Travel for p106(br), /©fancy for p109, /©Atlantide SNC for p111(t), /©Brand X for Pre-intermediate B R-3(t), /©PhotoDisc for Pre-intermediate B R-3(b); Pictures Colour Library/©David Tomlinson for p40(t); Punchstock/©Valueline for p7(bcr), /©Glowimages for p31(b), /©Valueline for p48(br), /©Corbis for p52(tcl), /©photosindia for p52(cr), /©Glowimages for p85(b), /©GoGo Images for p87(tl), /©Digital Vision for p102(cl), /©Cultura for p119(br), /©Comstock for Pre-intermediate A R-5(toast); Random House Inc for p36(r); Rex Features for p27(lb), /©Geoff Robinson for p33, /©Sipa Press for p60(t), /©Everett Collection for p60(c), /©Sky Magazine for p112(c); Ruben Gonzalez for p12(tl, tr); Science Museum for p112(t); Shutterstock/©David P Lewis for p9, /©Lana Langlois for p10(tcr), /©Smit for p32(A), /©spe for p32(B), /©Sandra Caldwell for p32(C), /©Sandra Caldwell for p32(D), /©HP_photo for p32(F), /©Stephen Coburn for p40(r), /©Margo for p52(tl), /©Ramzi Hachicho for p54(tr), /©Benis Arapovic for p54(bl), /©Rene Jansa for p55, /©Carsten Reisinger for p58(b), /©Ivana Rauski for p70(A), /©grzym for p70(C), /©Tootles for p70(C), /©Sergey Titov for p70(D), /Juriah Mosin for p75, /©MaxFX for p97, /©SF Photo for p99(t), /©Lee Torens for p106(tr), /©serg64 for p112(b), /©ultimathule for Pre-intermediate A R-5(basil), /©vinicius Tupinamba for Pre-intermediate A R-5(chicken), /©Joe Gough for Pre-intermediate A R-5(curry), /©Jan Hopgood for Pre-intermediate A R-5(fruit), /©Valda for Pre-intermediate A R-5(herbs), /©Joe Gough for Pre-intermediate A R-5(lasagne), /©luchschen for Pre-intermediate A R-5(mushrooms), /©stoupa for Pre-intermediate A R-5(strawberries), /©viktor1 for Pre-intermediate A R-5(bread), /©ZTS for Pre-intermediate A R-5(cake), /©ZTS for Pre-intermediate A R-5(cucumber), /©Sarune Zurbaite for Pre-intermediate A R-5(ice cream), /©Olga Lyubkina for Pre-intermediate A R-5(oil), /©ncn18 for Pre-intermediate A R-5(olives), /©Juha-Pekka Kervinen for Pre-intermediate A R-5(pasta), /©Anton Gvozdikov for Pre-intermediate A R-5(a pear), /©Robert Redelowski for Pre-intermediate A R-5(potatoes), /©Kentoh for Pre-intermediate A R-5(prawns), /©Tobik for Pre-intermediate A R-5(rice), /©Stuart Monk for Pre-intermediate A R-5(salmon), /©Chin Kit Sen for Pre-intermediate A R-5(soup), /©Joe Gough for Pre-intermediate A R-5(steak), /©Robyn Mackenzie for Pre-intermediate A R-5(tomatoes), /©Elke Dennis for 142(chop), /©3445128471 for Pre-intermediate A R-5(cut), /©iker canikligil for Pre-intermediate A R-5(pour); Stock Food UK for p32(tr,br); The Terem Quartet for p11(r); Topfoto/©Fortean for p68(c); www.judybevan.com for p27(r); www.sekwaman.co.za for p12(br); www.womadelaide.com for p11(l).

We have been unable to trace the copyright holder of the photographs on pp58(tl,tr), 69(b) and Pre-intermediate A R-3 and would welcome any information enabling us to do so.

The photograph on 28(tr) was kindly taken by an employee of the Melbourne Office, Cambridge University Press.

The following photographs were taken on commission by Gareth Boden for CUP:

7(bcl), 16, 22, 24(l), 28(bl), 42(l, r), 43, 48(bl), 54(tl), 56(cr), 62, 76(A, B, C, D), 78

We are grateful to the following for their help with the commissioned photography:

Fitzwilliam Museum, Cambridge; Greens Health & Fitness, Cambridge; Greg Sibley; Legal Moves, Hertford; Linda Matthews; Stephen Perse 6th Form College, Cambridge; The Lounge, Hertford; Thomas Cook, Cambridge.

Illustrations by Derek Bacon, Kathy Baxendale, Tom Croft, Mark Duffin, Kamae Design, Julian Mosedale, Mark Preston, Nigel Sanderson, Sean Simms.

Intro goals
- introduce and talk about yourself
- talk about needs, wants and reasons

Me and my life

I'm from Ottawa

1 Introduce yourself to your group.

the Rideau Canal, Ottawa

Hi, my name's Kate Mori. I'm from Ottawa in Canada.

Kate Mori

LISTENING

2 a Look at the pictures from Kate's life. What can you guess about her:

   1 family?   2 work?   3 free time?

b ⭐ 1.1 Listen to check your ideas.

VOCABULARY

Your life

3 Complete Kate's sentences. ⭐ 1.1 Listen again to check.

1 I live with *my husband, Masao.*	5 I speak ... 8 I like ...
2 We have ...	6 I'm studying ... 9 I play ...
3 I'm a ...	7 I'm interested in ... 10 I go ...
4 I work ...	

4 Add more words to each group.

family members	jobs	languages	study subjects	sports and hobbies
husband	teacher	English	art history	tennis

SPEAKING

5 a Think of five things to tell other students about yourself.

b Talk to each other in groups.

Ela's from Poland. She speaks Polish, English and Spanish.

6 How much can you remember about the people in your group?

I really want to ...

Kate from Canada

Sun-Hi from South Korea

Kemal from Turkey

Kate, Kemal and Sun-Hi are all learning languages.

LISTENING

1 a ▶ 1.2 Can you remember what language Kate is learning? Why do you think she's learning it? Listen to check.

b ▶ 1.2 Listen again. Does Kate learn at home or go to a class? Why?

2 a ▶ 1.3 Now listen to Kemal and Sun-Hi.

1 What languages are they learning?
2 Who's learning for work? Who's learning for fun?

b ▶ 1.3 Listen again. What exactly does each person want to do in the language?

3 Read the scripts on R-13 to check your answers in 1 and 2.

VOCABULARY

Needs, wants and reasons

4 Who says these things: Kate, Kemal or Sun-Hi?

1 I need English for my work. *Sun-Hi*
2 I sometimes need English for my studies.
3 I don't need English for travel.
4 I need to practise my writing.
5 One day I want to watch Spanish films.
6 I really want to talk with my husband's family.
7 I'd like to have a real conversation with them.
8 I'd really like to go to Spain.

5 Complete these sentences with because or so.

1 I'm learning Japanese *because* I want to talk with my husband's family.
2 I didn't want to stop studying, _____ I started going to classes.
3 I'm learning Spanish _____ I like it.
4 I have a job with an international company, _____ I need English for my work.

6 a Why are you learning English? Think about why you need it and what you'd like to do.

b Talk together. Which reasons are the most common and the most interesting?

> I need English for work because I travel a lot.

> I'd like to watch American films, so I need to improve my listening.

SPEAKING

7 a Read 1–8. Write questions.

Do you want to move to another city or town?

Find someone who:
1 wants to move to another city or town.
2 would like to change jobs.
3 always needs a coffee first thing in the morning.
4 likes modern art.
5 wants to run in a marathon.
6 would like to have more free time.
7 is interested in motorbikes.
8 goes to night school.

b Make two more questions for the people in your class.

8 a Talk to different people. Ask each other questions and use *because* or *so* to give reasons.

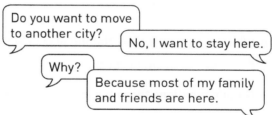

> Do you want to move to another city?

> No, I want to stay here.

> Why?

> Because most of my family and friends are here.

b In pairs, tell each other what you learned about the people in your class.

Self-assessment

Can you do these things in English? Circle a number on each line. 1 = I can't do this, 5 = I can do this well.

| ◉ introduce and talk about yourself | 1 2 3 4 5 |
| ◉ talk about needs, wants and reasons | 1 2 3 4 5 |

1 Play

1.1 goals
◉ talk about music
◉ talk about what to do in your free time

Local music

1 **Talk together.**

1 Do you listen to music a lot?
2 What types of music do you like?
3 Can you play any instruments?

Natalie talks about music in Trinidad and Tobago, where she grew up.

the steel drums

the piano

the guitar

2 **🔊 1.4 Listen to Natalie and answer the questions.**

1 Do people in Trinidad and Tobago only listen to local music, or music from around the world?
2 Which instruments in the pictures does Natalie talk about?

3 a Which instrument does Natalie play now? Which doesn't she play? Why?

b 🔊 1.4 Listen again to check.

4 a Natalie mentions these types of music. Can you think of any more?

Cuban music, reggae, classical, calypso, salsa, rumba ...

b What types of music are popular where you live?

5 Match 1–7 with a–g and complete the sentences from Natalie's interview.

1 I learned how to play the steel drum when
2 I would love to be able to
3 I was brought up to
4 Nowadays I play more
5 We have our own instrument called
6 We have a local music called
7 Calypso is similar to music from

a calypso.
b play classical piano.
c Cuban music.
d I was a little girl.
e Latin America.
f play it again.
g the steel drum.

6 Write four or five sentences about some of these things. Use the highlighted expressions from 5.

• music in your country • a special instrument in your country
• a type of music you like • music in your childhood
• music in your life now • something you'd like to learn

7 Talk to each other about music in your country and in your life. Ask questions to find out more.

I learned how to play the guitar when I was a teenager.

Were you in a band?

Music around the world

READING AND LISTENING

1 Read the online programme for WOMADelaide on Sunday. Do you know any of the performers? Which would you most like to see?

WOMADelaide BOTANIC PARK, ADELAIDE SUNDAY 12.00 — 6.00

WOMAD (World of Music, Arts and Dance) organises international music festivals in over twenty countries.

At WOMADelaide, you can enjoy the magical sounds of the planet in the sunshine with friends and family. (Kids under 12 are free.) Come for a night, a day, or for the whole three days.

Cesaria Evora – Cape Verde Cesaria Evora's beautiful songs are sung in Creole Portuguese and originate from traditional Portuguese and Brazilian music.

Toumani Diabate's Symmetric Orchestra – Mali More than any other kora player, Toumani Diabate has brought the unique 21-string West African harp to people around the world.

Mista Savona – Australia This 13-piece group – including some of Jamaica's best singers together with leading Australian musicians – brings a huge and exciting reggae sound to the stage.

The Beautiful Girls – Australia Singer-songwriter-guitarist Mat McHugh started The Beautiful Girls in 2002, but the band has changed a lot since then. Their music takes in hip-hop and reggae, soul and pop.

Terem Quartet – Russia Putting new life into Russian folk music, the Terem Quartet's performances are full of fun and incredible musical energy.

Terem Quartet

TIMES AND STAGES. • FULL LINE-UP. • SITE MAP.

2 🎵 **1.5** Listen to two friends at work, Cameron and John, talking about the programme. Which performers do they talk about? Which do they both want to see?

VOCABULARY
Deciding what to do

3 a Complete the sentences from the conversation with words from the box.

| see   have a look   good   idea   ~~go~~   get   into |

1 **JOHN** Do you want to __*go*__?
  CAMERON Sure, if we can get tickets for a day or a night.

2 **J** Why don't we _____ online?
  C OK, hang on a minute.

3 **J** Mista Savona looks interesting.
  C Hm, I'm not really _____ reggae.

4 **J** What do you think about this? The Terem Quartet?
  C The folk? Yeah, that sounds _____.

5 **J** Do you want me to _____ if there are any tickets?
  C Good _____.

6 **J** Maybe we could _____ a group together.
  C Yeah, it would be a good laugh.

b 🎵 **1.5** Listen again to check. ℗

4 Work in pairs. Take turns to say the first lines in 1–6 and remember the responses.

SPEAKING

5 a Work alone and choose:

  1 two performers from the programme that look interesting.
  2 two performers you don't want to see.

b In groups, decide:

  1 one performer you'd all like to see.
  2 who will book the tickets.
  3 where to meet.

6 Tell the class what you decided. Which are the most popular performers in the class? Which are the least popular?

An unusual athlete

1.2 goals
- talk about past events and present activities
- talk about sport and exercise

READING

1 Read the introduction to an interview. What's unusual about Ruben?

An interview with Ruben Gonzalez

At school, Argentina's Ruben Gonzalez was not a natural athlete. However, at the age of 21, he started doing the Olympic sport of luge and, four years later, he represented Argentina at the Calgary Winter Olympics. How did he do it?

▲ *Ruben today*

▲ *Ruben at the 2002 Winter Olympics*

2 Read the interview with Ruben on p13 and answer the questions.

1 Why did Ruben decide to become an Olympic athlete?
2 Why did he choose the luge?
3 How many Winter Olympics was he in?
4 What's his job now?

3 Read the interview again. Why is luge a difficult sport? Find three reasons.

4 What do you think about Ruben? What do you think about what he's done?

GRAMMAR

Present simple, past simple, present progressive

5 Complete 1–3 in the table with the correct time expression from the box.

| at the moment   ~~sometimes~~   in 1988 |

6 Now complete 4–9 with are, do, didn't, don't, 'm not, did.

	present simple	past simple	present progressive
⊕	I still practise on the luge ¹*sometimes* .	I went to the Olympics ² _____ .	I'm making a film ³ _____ .
❓	How often ⁴ _____ you practise?	When ⁵ _____ you go to the Olympics?	What ⁶ _____ you doing at the moment?
⊖	I ⁷ _____ practise at weekends.	I ⁸ _____ go in 1998.	I ⁹ _____ doing anything.

7 a Complete the questions with the correct form of the verb in (brackets).

1 What sport _did_ Ruben _play_ at school? (play)
2 Why _____ he _____ the luge? (choose)
3 When _____ luge athletes usually _____ training? (start)
4 How fast _____ a luge _____? (go)
5 How often _____ he _____? (practise)
6 What _____ he _____ these days? (do)

Grammar reference and practice, R-6

b Write two more questions to ask a partner about Ruben.

c How much can you remember? Ask and answer all the questions.

SPEAKING

8 a Look at the photos. What can you guess about the people?

b Work in A/B pairs. A, read about Michelle on R-1. B, read about Vincent on R-3. Follow the instructions.

c Tell each other about Michelle and Vincent.

Michelle Sung Wie

Vincent Mantsoe

Interviewer So, Ruben, how did you get into the luge?

Ruben Well, at school, I couldn't jump high or run fast. I played football but I wasn't very good. It was really sad! But when I was ten, I saw the Olympics on TV for the first time and I loved it. And later, when I was 21, I saw Scott Hamilton win an Olympic medal in figure skating. Scott's about 155 cm tall and weighs about 50 kilos, and he gave me hope. I thought: if that little guy can do it, I can do it too. So I decided to be an Olympic champion – but I had to find a sport. It's true, I'm not a great athlete, but I never give up. I try again and again. So I chose the luge because people get hurt a lot, people often break bones – ninety percent of them give up. And I thought, well, I don't give up, so I have a chance.

Interviewer Most Olympic luge athletes start training at 12. You started at 21, but you've competed in three Olympics.

Ruben Yes, I started in 1984. I went to the Winter Olympics in Calgary in 1988 and in Albertville in 1992. Then, nearly ten years later, my old coach phoned me up and said "Argentina needs you!" So at age 39, I competed in the 2002 Salt Lake City Winter Olympics.

Interviewer What's it like to luge down a mountain at 90 miles an hour?

Ruben Well, at that speed, you don't have time to think. The luge is very sensitive. If you hiccup, you can crash. And when you finish, you have to sit up and stop the luge by putting your feet on the ice. It takes a couple of hundred metres to stop because you finish the run at about 80 miles an hour. I still practise on the luge sometimes and I'm frightened on every run.

Interviewer And what do you do these days?

Ruben I'm a motivational speaker. I talk about my experiences and how to be successful. I'm making a film about success at the moment. We're interviewing a lot of business people, philosophers, athletes, Hollywood people. It's very interesting.

Physical activities

VOCABULARY
Sports and exercise

1 a Match the activities with the pictures A–I.

> aerobics   hockey   karate   running   skiing
> swimming   tennis   volleyball   yoga

b Match the activities with the verbs 1–3.

1   I play *hockey*   2   I do …   3   I go …

c Can you think of more activities for verbs 1–3?

PRONUNCIATION
Word stress

2 a How many syllables are there in the words in 1a? Where's the stress? Put the words in groups.

Oo ¹	Ooo ²	oOo ³
hockey		

b 🔊 1.6 Listen to check. ℗

SPEAKING

3 In groups, ask and answer the questions. Find out more.

1   What activities do you do?
2   What do you watch?
3   What did you do when you were younger?

> When I was at college, I did aerobics.
>> Did you like it?

Target activity

Talk about an interest

1.3 goals
- talk about past events and present activities ♻
- talk about your interests and how they started

Li from England

TASK LISTENING

1 Which of these things are you interested in? Why? Talk together.

fashion   books   motorbikes   cars   sports   computers   cooking   travel
art   history   music   photography   science   cinema   politics

2 🔊 **1.7** Listen to Li talking about her interest in motorbikes. Where does she like riding her motorbike?

3 **a** Can you remember what Li says about:

1   when she was a child and a teenager?
2   why she decided to start riding a motorbike?
3   her motorbike lessons?
4   what she likes about being on a motorbike?

b 🔊 **1.7** Listen again to check.

TASK VOCABULARY

Talking about interests

4 Make six sentences from the interview with Li. Which are about the past? Which are about now?

1	It started when	a	learn something new.
2	I really got into	b	going fast.
3	I really wanted to	c	I was a kid.
4	The great thing about it is,	d	motorbikes when I was a teenager.
5	I'm not interested in	e	it doesn't take very long to learn.
6	For me,	f	speed isn't important.

TASK

5 **a** Choose something you're really interested in. Think about these questions.

1   When and how did your interest start?
2   How did you feel about it when you started?
3   How do you feel about it now? Why do you like it?
4   How much time does it take? When do you do it? Where?

> I really got into cooking when I was a teenager

b Tell each other about your interests. Ask questions to find out more.

6 Would you like to try any of the things you talked about?

Keyword *so*

1 We use so before a result, like this:

> My first boyfriend had a really nice bike, so we went riding in the countryside a lot. *Unit 1*

Add so to the correct place in each sentence.

so
1 I thought, well, I don't give up ∧ I have a chance. *Unit 1*
2 A steel drum's about a metre high I couldn't really travel with it. *Unit 1*
3 I have a job with a large international company I need English for my work. *Intro unit*
4 Masao's interested in art too we usually go to galleries together. *Intro unit*

2 a What important decisions have you made in the last five years? Write three sentences with so.

I wanted a better job, so I started studying at the local college.

> What did you study?

b Listen to each other's sentences. Ask questions to find out more.

3 Make four conversations and then practise in pairs. Take turns to say 1–4 and remember a–d.

1 Do you need to work late tonight?   a Yes, I think so, but Casablanca's much bigger.
2 Do you think it'll rain tomorrow?   b I'm really tired but yes, I suppose so / I guess so.
3 What's the capital of Morocco? Is it Rabat?   c I hope so. This weather's too hot for me.
4 Do you think the bank's open now?   d No, I don't think so. They usually close at four.

4 a Write three questions for a partner about these topics.
Use: Do you think ... ?

> Do you think chocolate is good for you?
>
> I hope so. I eat lots of it!

- food and drink • sport • music • the weather • free time

b Ask and answer the questions. Try to use the expressions in 3.

Across cultures Culture shock

1 a What do you think happens when people move to a new country or culture? Make three sentences.

1 At first   a life is difficult and you miss your home.
2 After a few days or weeks   b you start living normally.
3 After a while   c you think everything is great.

b Read the article to check. Do you agree with the ideas?

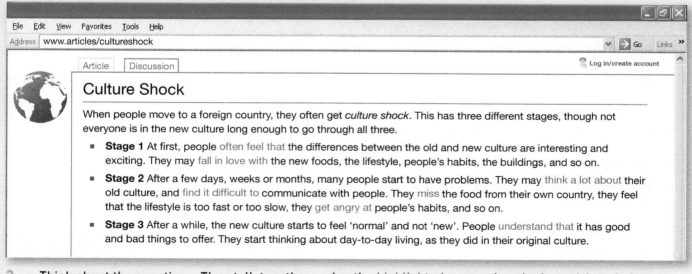

File   Edit   View   Favorites   Tools   Help

Address www.articles/cultureshock

Article | Discussion   Log in/create account

Culture Shock

When people move to a foreign country, they often get *culture shock*. This has three different stages, though not everyone is in the new culture long enough to go through all three.

- **Stage 1** At first, people often feel that the differences between the old and new culture are interesting and exciting. They may fall in love with the new foods, the lifestyle, people's habits, the buildings, and so on.

- **Stage 2** After a few days, weeks or months, many people start to have problems. They may think a lot about their old culture, and find it difficult to communicate with people. They miss the food from their own country, they feel that the lifestyle is too fast or too slow, they get angry at people's habits, and so on.

- **Stage 3** After a while, the new culture starts to feel 'normal' and not 'new'. People understand that it has good and bad things to offer. They start thinking about day-to-day living, as they did in their original culture.

2 Think about the questions. Then talk together, using the highlighted expressions in the article to help you.

1 Have you (or people you know) ever had culture shock? What happened?
2 What things do people usually like when they come to your country? What things can be difficult for them?
3 Have you ever gone to live, work or study in a new place? Would you like to?
4 What things were new for you? How did you feel about them? Did you get used to them?

1 EXPLORE**Writing**

1 Look at the photo. What's wrong with Cameron? How do you think he feels?

2 a Read the emails.

1 What will Cameron do for the next few days? Why?
2 What are the names of: his friends? his client?
3 What does he arrange to do next week?

b Which emails are more formal? Which are less formal?

3 a What expressions do Cameron, Marc and Pam use to begin and end their emails? Make two lists.

Beginning (x4): *Dear Marc* , ...
Ending (x5): *Regards, Cameron Clarke* ...

b Which expressions from 3a would you use when writing to these people? Compare your ideas.

- someone in your family   • a friend
- your manager   • a client
- someone you don't know

4 a Cover the emails. Can you complete the sentences with these expressions?

~~Any time~~   drop by   changing our appointment
give me a call   take a few days off
If so   over lunch

Requests

1 Would you mind _____ to Monday or Tuesday next week? _Any time_ is fine.
2 When you see John, could you tell him to _____?
3 Is it all right if I _____ tomorrow, or would you prefer to be alone?

Invitations

4 Would you like to join me at Chez Michel at one o'clock? We could talk about the project _____ .
5 Do you want to meet up this evening – barbecue maybe? _____ let me know.
6 I have to _____. How about dinner next week?

b Look at the emails to check.

5 Write short emails for these situations.

1 Invite a friend to meet you somewhere. Give the date, time and place.
2 Cancel an appointment with a client. Give the reason, suggest a new time, and invite her / him to lunch.

6 Exchange emails with a partner. Write a short reply to each one.

7 Look at all your emails together. Do you think they have the correct style?

Goal

write messages of request and invitation to different people

Dear Marc,
I'm very sorry but I have to cancel our appointment for today. I'm not well. Would you mind changing our appointment to Monday or Tuesday next week? Any time is fine.
Regards,
Cameron Clarke

Hello Cameron,
I'm sorry to hear you're not feeling well. Tuesday next week is fine with me. Would you like to join me at Chez Michel at one o'clock? We could talk about the project over lunch. Get well soon.
Best wishes,
Marc

Hi Cameron,
Do you want to meet up this evening – barbecue maybe? If so, let me know. John and Jen are coming too.
Love, Pam

Delete Reply Reply All Forward Print

Pam,
Really sorry but I woke up this morning with a cold and feel terrible. I have to take a few days off. How about dinner next week?
Cameron.

PS When you see John, could you tell him to give me a call?

You poor thing! Yes, next week will be good. Is it all right if I drop by tomorrow, or would you prefer to be alone? Take care, P :-)

1 Look again ♻

Review

1 a Work together. How many words or expressions can you think of:

1 connected with music? *jazz, instrument ...*
2 for sports and exercise? *swimming, yoga ...*

b 🔊 **1.8** Listen to eight instructions. Write down your answers – but don't write them in order.

c Look at each other's answers. Can you guess what they mean?

> Wrestling ... Do you like watching wrestling on TV?
>
> No, I hate it!

GRAMMAR Question patterns

2 a Put the words in order. Write the questions in the table.

1 like do What you doing in the evening?
2 Can ride you a motorbike?
3 did Where go you to school?
4 reading you Are anything interesting at the moment?
5 you would What places like to visit in future?

Question word	Auxiliary verb	Subject	Verb	
1 *What*	*do*	*you*	*like*	*doing in the evening?*
2 –	*Can*	...	...	...

b Write two more questions to ask a partner. Then ask and answer all the questions.

CAN YOU REMEMBER? Intro unit – Needs, wants

3 a Complete the conversations with 'd like, want, need.

1 A I can't find my bank card.
  B I think you _____ to phone the bank.
2 A Hello. Can I get you something?
  B Yes, I _____ some cake and a coffee, please.
3 A Shall we go out tonight?
  B No, I _____ / _____ to stay at home. There's a good film on TV.

b Write sentences about things you'd like, want or need to do:

• after this lesson • tomorrow
• next weekend • next week • next year

c Listen to each other's sentences. Give more information.

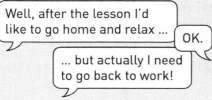

> Well, after the lesson I'd like to go home and relax ...
>
> OK.
>
> ... but actually I need to go back to work!

Extension

SPELLING AND SOUNDS *or, wor-*

4 a 🔊 **1.9** Listen and repeat the words with or and wor-.

or with stress /ɔː/	*or* without stress /ə/	*wor-* /wɜː/
spórt bórn	motórbike dóctor	work

b Add these words to the correct group. Practise saying them.

forget morning word
orchestra visitor world

c 🔊 **1.10** Spellcheck. Close your book. Listen to ten words with or and wor- and write them down.

d Look at the script on R-14 to check your spelling.

NOTICE Extreme adjectives

5 a Find the adjectives in this unit which mean:

1 really good, special: m*agical*, u_____e, i_____e.
  (the festival programme on p11)
2 really nice: l_____y.
  (Natalie's script on R-13)
3 really good, great: a_____g
  (Cameron and John's conversation on R-13)
4 really interesting: f_____g
5 really frightening: t_____g
6 really bad: t_____e
  (the interview with Li on R-13–R-14)

b Think about how to describe some things and people you really like or don't like, for example:

• a musician • a book • a TV programme
• a sportsperson • a film • a politician
• a place • an activity

c Tell each other your ideas. Do you agree?

Self-assessment

Can you do these things in English? Circle a number on each line. 1 = I can't do this, 5 = I can do this well.

⊙ talk about music	1	2	3	4	5
⊙ talk about what to do in your free time	1	2	3	4	5
⊙ talk about sport and exercise	1	2	3	4	5
⊙ talk about past events and present activities	1	2	3	4	5
⊙ talk about your interests and how they started	1	2	3	4	5
⊙ write messages of request and invitation to different people	1	2	3	4	5

• For Wordcards, reference and saving your work » e-Portfolio
• For more practice » Self-study Pack, Unit 1

2

2.1 goals
- talk about personal experience
- talk about your studies

Work and studies

Lifelong learning

1 **Ask and answer the questions.**

1 At what age do people in your country usually do these things?
- start school • go to college or university • do exams
- do military service • start work • retire
2 What do you think are the best ages to do them?

2 **Read the introduction to a radio programme. Is this true of people where you live?**

In today's programme, we'll be taking a look at lifelong learning. In the past, people went to school and maybe university, then they got a job and that was it. Today, however, all that is changing. Many people are continuing to study all their lives and some are going back to school or university when they are much older.

Luis

Pierre

Margaret

3 **1.11 Listen to interviews with three students, Luis, Pierre and Margaret.**

1 Match them with pictures A–C.
2 Who:
   a started studying after they retired?
   b works and studies at the same time?
   c went to college after working for 20 years?

A

B

C

4 **a Can you remember the answers to these questions?**

Luis	1	What does he do?	2	What are his plans for the future?
Pierre	3	Why didn't he like school?	4	Why does he enjoy his studies now?
Margaret	5	Why did she join the U3A?	6	How is the U3A different from other universities?

b 1.11 Listen again to check.

5 **Do you know anyone with similar stories to Luis, Pierre or Margaret? Talk together.**

6 a Who mentions these subjects? What do they say about them?

Spanish IT skills archaeology history maths science music art

b In groups, add more subjects to the list. Then compare as a class.

geography, French ...

exams
a degree
a thesis
an IT skills course
colleges
a ~~doctorate~~
courses
degrees
School

7 a Complete the sentences from the interviews with words or expressions from the box.

1 I'm doing _a doctorate_ in archaeology.
2 I'm writing _____ on my work in the Amazon.
3 I passed my _____ – just!
4 I wanted to do _____ in art.
5 I applied to some _____ .
6 I got into the _____ of Art and Design in Limoges.
7 We don't do exams or get _____ .
8 I've done _____ in music, local history and Spanish.
9 Last week I signed up for _____ .

b Which words in the box in 7a can go with these verbs?   do   get   pass / fail

do a degree, do a doctorate ...

8 Write five sentences about your past or present studies. Use the expressions in 7a.

SPEAKING **9** Listen to each other's sentences. Ask questions to find out more.

> Last year I did a course in marketing.   Where did you do it?

I've done ...

GRAMMAR

Present perfect 1 – for experience

1 Look at the sentences from the interview with Pierre and answer the questions.

1 I've always enjoyed art.   2 I didn't like a lot of subjects at school.

In which sentence is he talking about: **a** only the past?   **b** his whole life up to now?

2 a Complete the sentences with have, has, 've, haven't, hasn't.

have / has + past participle	
❓ What kind of courses _____ you done? ➕ I've done courses in music, local history and Spanish. ➖ I choose things I _____ studied before. ➖ I _____ never been very good with computers.	Has she ever studied Spanish? Yes, she _____ . No, she _____ .

b [1.12] Listen to check. ℗

3 Complete the questions with the past participles of the verbs in (brackets).

1 What subjects have you always _enjoyed_? (enjoy)
2 What subjects have you always _____ good at? (be)
3 What's the most useful subject you've ever _____? (study)
4 Who's the best teacher you've ever _____? (have)
5 Have you ever _____ a course in your free time? (do)
6 Have you ever _____ a thesis or a very long essay? (write)
7 Have you _____ a lot of exams in your life? (do)
8 What's the most difficult exam you've ever _____? (pass)

You can look up irregular past participles on R-22, *Irregular verbs*.

Grammar reference and practice, R-7

PRONUNCIATION

Sentence stress **4 a** [1.13] We stress the most important words in a sentence (often question words, nouns, verbs, adjectives and adverbs). Listen to these questions from 3 and practise.

1 What subjects have you always enjoyed?
2 What subjects have you always been good at?

b Look at the other questions in 3. Decide which words should be stressed and underline them. [1.14] Then listen and compare.

SPEAKING **5** Ask and answer the questions in 3. Ask questions to find out more.

> I've always loved maths.   Why? Did you have good teachers at school?

A great place to work?

2.2 goals
- talk about personal experience ♻
- talk about your work

SPEAKING

1 **a** Use the work quiz to interview each other.
Give reasons for your answers.

The work quiz

What would be your ideal job? Would you prefer to:

1 (a) work for a big company? ☐ (b) work for a small company? ☐
(c) be self-employed? ☐

2 (a) have a full-time job? ☐ (b) have a part-time job? ☐
(c) work whenever you want? ☐

3 (a) work in an office? ☐ (b) work outdoors? ☐ (c) work at home? ☐

4 (a) work alone? ☐ (b) work with the same people every day? ☐
(c) often work with different people? ☐

5 (a) have a well-paid job? ☐ (b) have an interesting job? ☐
(c) have a job which helps other people? ☐

b For each question 1–5, what's the most common answer in the class?
Are your reasons the same?

READING

2 Read four web postings by people who work for CSP, a company which designs
and sells computer software. Who's generally happy at CSP? Who's not happy?

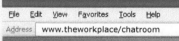

File Edit View Favorites Tools Help

Address www.theworkplace/chatroom ⌄ → Go Links »

The Workplace > chat

1 Posted by: Marco

I've worked here since 2008 when I left college and I quite like it. I work in the IT department and there's a nice atmosphere. Everyone's easy to work with, friendly – it's a bit like a family really. I'm always busy but we have flexible working hours: sometimes I'm here from 7 to 3, sometimes from 10 to 6. That's good when you've been out the night before! The pay's good too. <u>View 2 replies to this comment</u>

2 Posted by: noname99

I've only worked here for a couple of months but I already hate it. The people in IT never seem to do any work. There's one young guy who's always late, and that can be really difficult. The management isn't very good either. They don't listen to you and they're often not here or too busy to talk. So basically, it's a terrible place to work and I'm looking for a new job. <u>View 3 replies to this comment</u>

3 Posted by: Lauren101

I've been with the sales team at CSP for three months and it's a great place to work. My boss is the best – she's never here, always away on business trips! But seriously, the atmosphere here's pretty relaxed because we often don't have a lot to do, and we probably spend a bit too much time surfing the Internet and having long lunch breaks. The pay's not great, but it's enough for now. <u>View 10 replies to this comment</u>

4 Posted by: Lydia

I started working here about three years ago. The job's interesting but it can be quite stressful because I work with the sales team. They make a lot of mistakes, and then I have to fix them. The pay's not great – I never have any money at the end of the month! But the benefits are OK – I get four weeks' holiday a year and free health care. <u>No replies to this comment</u>

3 Read the postings again. Who:

1 is in the sales team?
2 sometimes has problems because of the sales team?
3 is in the IT department?
4 isn't happy with the IT department?
5 doesn't have a lot of work?
6 came to CSP after college?
7 wants to leave CSP?
8 doesn't say anything about money?

4 Who do you think would be good to work with? Who could be difficult to work with? Why?

VOCABULARY

Working conditions

5 Complete statements 1–6. Then read the postings again to check.

1 We have flexible working hours:
2 The management isn't very good either.
3 The benefits are OK –
4 The pay's not great –
5 It's a terrible place to work
6 There's a nice atmosphere.

a I never have any money at the end of the month!
b I get four weeks' holiday a year and free health care.
c They don't listen to you.
d and I'm looking for a new job.
e Everyone's easy to work with.
f sometimes I'm here from 7 to 3, sometimes from 10 to 6.

SPEAKING

What's your job like?

It's great, because we have flexible working hours ...

6 a Think about how to describe some of these things with the expressions in 5.

1 your job now   2 jobs in your past   3 jobs of people you know

b Talk together.

I've worked here for ...

GRAMMAR

Present perfect 2 – with *for* and *since*

1 Look at the sentences from the postings.

> *Marco* I've worked here since 2008.
> *Lauren101* I've been with the sales team at CSP for three months.

1 When did Marco and Lauren start working at CSP?
2 Do they work there now?
3 Complete a and b with for and since:

a You can use _____ to say when something started (Monday, last month, 2008).
b You can use _____ with a period of time (a week, three months, five years).

2 a Write four sentences about yourself on a piece of paper. Use the ideas below with *for* and *since*. Then give your sentences to your teacher.

I've worked at ...   I've been a ...   I've lived in ...
I've known ...   I've studied ...   I've had my ...

I've worked at my present company for about five years.

Grammar reference and practice, R-7

b Listen to each set of sentences. Can you guess who wrote them?

SPEAKING

You've been a teacher for five years, right?

No, only two.

Oh, sorry, two years. What do you teach?

3 Talk in groups. What can you remember about each other from 2? Ask questions to find out more.

21

Target activity

Have an interview

2.3 goals
- talk about personal experience ♻
- talk about your studies ♻
- talk about your work ♻

Let **Findajob** help you find your dream job. Simply give us your CV and come in for an interview and we'll find the best job for someone with your skills and interests. You'll get experience with some of the world's best organisations and have the freedom to work how you want to. We can find you a job with a permanent or temporary contract and you can work full-time or part-time – the choice is yours!

TASK LISTENING

1 Read the advert for a job agency.

1 Do many people use job agencies where you live?
2 What are the advantages and disadvantages of using a job agency?
3 Have you or people you know ever used a job agency?

2 ▸ 1.15 Listen to part of Lauren's interview. In what order does the interviewer ask about these things?

☐ experience in sales
1 qualifications in catering
☐ strengths and weaknesses
☐ languages
☐ computer skills
☐ driving licence

Lauren Gordon has left CSP and is looking for a new job. She has an interview at the Findajob agency.

3 a Can you remember if these sentences are true or false? Lauren:

1 brings her CV with her. *true*
2 only wants to work in catering.
3 has her Food Safety certificate with her.
4 speaks some French and Spanish.
5 left CSP because she wasn't happy there.
6 says she has no weaknesses.

b ▸ 1.15 Listen again to check.

TASK VOCABULARY

Presenting yourself

4 a What does Lauren say in her interview? Match 1–8 with a–h.

1 I've got experience in
2 I'm looking for work in
3 I've got a certificate in
4 I've been in
5 I've always wanted to
6 I'm good at
7 I really enjoy
8 I'm not very good at

a work for a big company.
b Food Safety for Catering.
c talking to people, I think.
d working in a team.
e any of those areas, really.
f sales, administration and catering.
g sales for a year now.
h working on my own.

b Look at the script on R-14 to check.

c Use the highlighted expressions in 4a to write five sentences about yourself.

TASK

5 a Work in A/B pairs.

A, you've got an interview with Findajob. Think of answers to questions 1–5.
B, you're the interviewer. Write two more questions.

1 What experience have you got?
2 What kind of work are you looking for?
3 What qualifications have you got?
4 What languages can you speak?
5 What are your strengths and weaknesses?

b Interview your partner. Then change roles and do the interview again.

6 Were you happy with your interview? Why / Why not? Talk together.

Keyword *for*

1 a Look at the highlighted expressions in sentences 1–4 from this unit. Match them with explanations a–d.

> 1 I've only worked here **for a couple of months**.
> 2 Simply give us your CV and come in **for an interview**.
> 3 You worked **for Café Concerto** last summer.
> 4 I'm sure we'll have something **for you**.

a You can use *for* to give a reason, to answer *Why?*
b You can use *for* with a time period.
c You can use *for* to say who receives something.
d You use *for* after some verbs (*ask, look, wait, work,* etc.).

b Now match more examples from the box with a–d.

> 1 I'm looking **for** a new job. Unit 2
> 2 Come **for** a night, a day, or **for** the whole three days. Unit 1
> 3 Do you use your bike **for** getting around, getting to work … ? Unit 1
> 4 Last year I wrote a book **for** children. Unit 1
> 5 I need English **for** my work. Intro unit

2 a Which sentence talks about a time period:
a in the past?   b in the future?   c up to now?

1 I've been in sales for a year.
2 Next year, I'm going to work in Brazil for the summer.
3 When I was a student, I went to university in Paris for nine months.

b Write three sentences like 1–3 about you. Then listen to each other's sentences and ask questions to find out more.

3 Put the words in order to make questions. Then ask and answer them in groups.

1 make / your friends / Do you ever / for / things / ?
   Do you ever make things for your friends?
2 your mobile phone / taking photos / for / use / Do you ever / ?
3 organised / someone / Have you ever / a party / for / ?
4 How often / you / for / do / buy tickets / or other events / concerts / ?
5 for / What websites / you / your work / do / use / or studies / ?
6 someone / the last time / for / a present / bought / you / When was / ?

Independent learning Noticing and recording collocations

1 a *Collocations* are words that often go together. Cross out the word that doesn't usually go with the highlighted words.

1 do / ~~make~~ / pass / fail **an exam**
2 a part-time / well-paid / happy / difficult **job**
3 a lunch / breakfast / coffee / cigarette **break**

b Which of the collocations are: adjective + noun?   verb + noun?   noun + noun?

2 Work in three groups. Complete the collocations with words from the postings on p20. Then show them to the other groups.

Group A, find adjectives:	Group B, find verbs:	Group C, find nouns:
a *nice* atmosphere	_____ mistakes	the _____ department
a _____ place to work	_____ the Internet	the _____ team
a _____ place to work	_____ a break	a _____ trip

3 a Look at three ways of recording collocations. Can you think of more ways?

Studies
go to university
pass an exam
fail an exam
write a thesis

Unit 2
We have <u>flexible working hours</u>.
horario de trabajo es flexible
I get <u>free health care</u>.
asistencia sanitaria gratuita

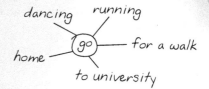

dancing   running
go
home — for a walk
to university

b Which do you prefer? Choose ways to record the collocations in 1a and 2.

1 a 🔊 1.16 **Listen to the phone call and choose a, b or c.**

1 The caller's name is
   a Clare.
   b Lisa Moore.
   c Yusuf Karim.
2 The person he needs to speak to is
   a at lunch.
   b in a meeting.
   c on holiday.
3 The caller leaves his
   a mobile number.
   b home number.
   c home address.
4 He wants Lisa Moore to
   a email him.
   b phone him.
   c send him something.

b Read the conversation to check.

2 a Read the conversation again. Which highlighted expressions:

1 ask someone to slow down? (x1)
2 ask someone to say something again? (x3)
3 ask someone to spell something? (x1)
4 show you understand? (x3)

b 🔊 1.17 **Listen to check.** Ⓟ

3 a Put the words in order to make sentences or questions about taking messages.

1 take you Would me message to like a ?
2 name again What your was please ?
3 would like to tell you What me her ?
4 message give her I'll the .
5 ask you her to I'll contact .

b Read the conversation to check.

4 a Cover the conversation. Role-play a similar conversation in A/B pairs.

A, you're Clare from CSP.
B, you're Yusuf Karim from Findajob (telephone 0412 556 207, email y.karim@findajob.com.au).

Try to use the highlighted **expressions in 2 and 3.**

b Change roles and practise again.

5 a Make two new phone calls in A/B pairs.

A, you work for CSP. Read role card 1 on R-1.
B, you work for Findajob. Read role card 2 on R-4.
Start the call.

b Change roles.

B, you work for CSP. Read role card 4 on R-4.
A, you work for Findajob. Read role card 3 on R-1.
Start the call.

Goals
- ask people to repeat, spell things and slow down
- show you understand
- take a phone message

A manager at the Findajob agency calls CSP to ask about their ex-employee, Lauren Gordon.

CLARE	Hello, CSP, Clare speaking. How can I help you?
YUSUF	Oh hello, my name's Yusuf Karim. I'm from the job agency, Findajob. Could I speak to Lisa Moore, please?
CLARE	Certainly. Can I ask you the reason for the call?
YUSUF	Of course. I'm calling about an ex-CSP employee, Lauren Gordon. Lisa Moore was her manager.
CLARE	Thank you. Let me just see if Lisa's available. Hello? I'm afraid she's in a meeting. Can I take a message?
YUSUF	I'm sorry, this line's not very good. Could you say that again, please?
CLARE	Yes, of course, I'm sorry. Would you like me to take a message?
YUSUF	Yes, please.
CLARE	Er, what was your name again, please?
YUSUF	Yes, it's Yusuf Karim.
CLARE	*Could you spell that for me?*
YUSUF	Yes, it's Yusuf with a Y, Y-U-S-U-F, and Karim is K-A-R-I-M.
CLARE	OK. And what's your telephone number?
YUSUF	I'll give you my mobile number. It's 0412 556 207.
CLARE	Sorry, can you speak more slowly, please?
YUSUF	Yes, it's 0412 556 207.
CLARE	Right. And has Lisa got your email address?
YUSUF	Er, no. It's y.karim@findajob.com.au.
CLARE	Sorry, y.karim@ … ?
YUSUF	Findajob – that's one word – dot com dot au.
CLARE	OK, so that's y.karim@findajob.com.au. And what would you like me to tell her?
YUSUF	Well, I'd like to ask her some questions about Lauren Gordon, what was she like as an employee and things. It would be great if she could phone me.
CLARE	OK, I'll give her the message and ask her to contact you.
YUSUF	Thank you. That's very helpful.
CLARE	No problem. Goodbye.

2 Look again ♻

Review

1 a Read the 'Find someone who' sentences below. Write four more like these for the people in your class.

> Find someone who:
> • has had the same job for more than two years.
> • has always liked the same music.
> • has worked for more than three companies.

b Make questions from the sentences, then ask them. Find out more details.

> Have you always liked the same music?

c Talk in groups. What did you find out about other people in the class?

VOCABULARY Working conditions

2 a Use the expressions to complete Fleur's posting. Is she happy in her job?

> flexible working hours   pay   free health care
> ~~easy to work with~~   benefits   management
> atmosphere

> **Posted by: Fleur89**
>
> The job's a bit boring, but the people are
> ¹*easy to work with* and there's a really good
> ²_____ in the office. The ³_____ aren't bad – I
> get ⁴_____ – but the ⁵_____ is terrible! I haven't
> had a rise since I started. We don't have ⁶_____
> – we start at eight in the morning and often work
> late. But the ⁷_____ is quite good. My boss is
> great and tells me conditions will get better if I
> stay here longer.

b Write a posting like Fleur's about your job or the job of someone you know.

CAN YOU REMEMBER? Unit 1 – Music, sports and exercise

3 a Use verbs from the box to complete the questions.

> done   go (x2)   listen to   ~~play~~

1 Can you _play_ volleyball?
2 Do you ever _____ running?
3 How often do you _____ to concerts?
4 Do you ever _____ classical music?
5 Have you ever _____ yoga?

b Think of two more endings for each question.

> *1 Can you play the guitar?*
> *Can you play football?*

c Ask and answer all the questions in 3a and b.

Extension

4 a ♦♦ 1.18 You say the endings -er, -or, -ar, -our in the same way, /ə/. Listen and repeat.

-er	-or	-ar	-our
lawy**er**	visit**or**	gramm**ar**	neighb**our**

b Complete these words with the correct endings. Practise saying them.

teach**er**   direct__   danc__
act__   sug__   behavi__

c ♦♦ 1.19 Spellcheck. Listen to ten more words and write them down.

d Look at the script on R-15 to check your spelling.

NOTICE Collocations

5 a Complete the highlighted collocations from the radio interviews with Pierre and Margaret.

> ask   free   got   great   have   IT   ~~left~~   passed

1 I __*left*__ school when I was eighteen. I _____ my exams – just! – and then I _____ a job.
2 It's a _____ experience, completely different from school.
3 I'm a lot older ... so it's easier to _____ questions, talk to the teachers, things like that.
4 We _____ meetings and talks in members' homes.
5 I retired three years ago. I had a lot of _____ time, and nothing to do.
6 Last week I signed up for an _____ skills course.

b Look at script 1.11 on R-14 to check.

c Choose three collocations and write questions with them.

> *Do you have a lot of meetings where you work?*

d Ask and answer your questions.

> ## Self-assessment
>
> Can you do these things in English? Circle a number on each line. 1 = I can't do this, 5 = I can do this well.
>
> | | | | | | |
> |---|---|---|---|---|---|
> | ◉ talk about personal experience | 1 | 2 | 3 | 4 | 5 |
> | ◉ talk about your studies | 1 | 2 | 3 | 4 | 5 |
> | ◉ talk about your work | 1 | 2 | 3 | 4 | 5 |
> | ◉ ask people to repeat, spell things and slow down | 1 | 2 | 3 | 4 | 5 |
> | ◉ show you understand | 1 | 2 | 3 | 4 | 5 |
> | ◉ take a telephone message | 1 | 2 | 3 | 4 | 5 |
>
> • For Wordcards, reference and saving your work » e-Portfolio
> • For more practice » Self-study Pack, Unit 2

3

How's your food?

Supermarkets or small shops?

VOCABULARY
Giving opinions

1 Look at the pictures. In groups, ask and answer the questions.

1 How often do you shop at places like these?
2 In your home, who does the food shopping?

2 Read three people's opinions about supermarkets. Do they like or dislike them? Why?

> " I think small shops are better. The owners are usually friendly and you can ask them about things. I find supermarkets quite stressful. They're always crowded and noisy. If you ask me, they're only interested in making money, not in their customers. "
>
> *Jenny, New Zealand*

> " Well, supermarkets are cheap and convenient but I prefer convenience stores. They're fast and modern and sell interesting things. Also, supermarkets bring a lot of their stuff here by plane and that's bad for the environment. They should sell more local food.
>
> *Akio, Japan*

> " I go to the market near my flat every day to buy food – things like meat, fish and vegetables. I never buy things like that in the supermarket. I don't think their food is fresh. But I guess they're good for cleaning products, pet food and so on. "
>
> *Luz, Spain*

3 Match the beginnings and endings of the opinions. Then look at 2 to check.

1 I think small shops   a sell more local food.
2 I find supermarkets   b cleaning products and pet food and so on.
3 If you ask me,   c are better.
4 They should   d is fresh.
5 I don't think their food   e quite stressful.
6 I guess they're good for   f they're only interested in making money.

4 a Find the opposites of these adjectives in 2.

> unfriendly *friendly* expensive relaxing inconvenient
> quiet boring empty old-fashioned

b 🔊 1.20 Listen to check. ℗

SPEAKING

5 a Think about places where people buy food in your country. What are their good and bad points?

b Listen to each other's opinions in groups. Say if you agree or disagree and give reasons.

> I think supermarkets are only good for people with cars.
>
> Yes, I agree.
>
> Well, I don't agree. I think ...

Food and you

READING

tinned food

frozen food

fresh fruit and vegetables

ready-made meals

1 Look at the pictures. Which kinds of food do you prefer to buy? Why?

2 Read the article by Judi Bevan. Which paragraphs:

a are about supermarkets now?   c compare shopping in the past and present?
b are about shopping in the past?

In defence of supermarkets

¹ I like supermarkets. I can buy a week's shopping in ninety minutes, giving me time to help my daughter with her homework, or read a good book in the bath.

² Supermarkets sell an amazing choice of fresh and frozen food. If I want to spend hours cooking a three-course dinner for friends, I can find all the ingredients I need at my local supermarket. If I choose an Italian meal, there are porcini mushrooms, fresh basil and mozzarella cheese. If I want some other cuisine – Indian, Chinese or French – herbs, spices, sauces and vegetables from every continent are only a few minutes away.

³ On the other hand, when I'm tired and just want to put together a quick family meal, I can buy a ready-made lasagne or curry, a bag of salad and some fresh fruit – and start eating it ten minutes after I get home.

⁴ Thanks to supermarkets, I can now shop all day from early morning to late at night. In some stores I can even shop 24 hours.

⁵ When I was a child, my mother didn't have these choices, as she went to three or four depressing little shops every day to buy what she needed. These shops opened from 9 am to 5 pm Monday to Saturday, and they all closed on Thursday afternoons.

⁶ The food was not always good, there was almost no choice and the shopkeepers were not very friendly. And at that time, food was very expensive. Cream on strawberries was a luxury, and roast chicken was for special occasions only.

⁷ Not many people would say that shopping in their local supermarket on a crowded Saturday morning makes them happy. But it's much, much better than what we had before.

Judi Bevan is a freelance financial journalist, author and broadcaster. Her books include *Trolley Wars – the Battle of the Supermarkets*, published in 2006.

3 Read the article again. Find four reasons why Judi likes supermarkets and four problems with shopping in the past.

4 Judi describes supermarkets in the UK. Which things are true about supermarkets in your country? Which things are different?

VOCABULARY
Food and meals

5 Add vowels to make food words from the article. Then look at the article to check. Look on R-5 to check any words you don't know.

1 bsl *basil*	4 vgtbls	7 strwbrrs	10 lsgn	13 mshrms
2 chs	5 crry	8 hrbs	11 sld	14 crm
3 spcs	6 frt	9 scs	12 chckn	

6 Match the examples from the box with a–d. Think of two more examples each for a–d.

> basil   dessert   lasagne   breakfast

a a meal   b a course   c an ingredient   d a dish

SPEAKING

7 In groups, ask and answer the questions. Find out more information.

1 Do you have a favourite kind of food, dish, or meal of the day?
2 What dishes can you, or people you know, cook? What ingredients do you use a lot?
3 Where you live, are there any good places to buy food from other countries?

I never eat mushrooms.

Why not? I love them!

Eating out

3.2 goals
- talk about food and eating ♻
- order a meal in a restaurant

READING AND LISTENING

1 Talk together.

1 How often do you go to cafés or restaurants?
2 Are there any good places to eat near your home?

2 a Read the information from a guide to eating out in Melbourne, Australia. Which restaurant:

1 is owned by a family?
2 has tables outside?

3 is open on Sundays?
4 sometimes has live music?

b Which of these restaurants would you like to go to? Why?

food&drink

The Bridge Restaurant

45 Hardware Lane, Melbourne Vic 3000
☎ *03 9600 234*

★★★★☆

The Bridge has a modern dining room serving quality European food. There is also a beautiful terrace for outdoor dining, and live jazz every Friday. Bookings essential. *Open Monday–Friday 12 pm – 10 pm, Saturday 5 pm – 10 pm.*

Bopha Devi Docklands

27 Rakaia Way, Docklands Vic 3008
☎ *03 9600 187*

★★★★☆

The new place in Docklands that everyone's talking about. The Bopha Devi Cambodian restaurant combines fantastic food with excellent service. *Open 12 pm – 11 pm. Closed Mondays.*

Abla's Lebanese Restaurant

109 Elgin Street, Carlton Vic 3053
☎ *03 9347 006*

★★★★☆

Choose from an exciting menu of Middle Eastern food, then sit back and enjoy the friendly service in this family-owned restaurant. *Open Thursday–Friday 12pm – 3pm, Monday–Saturday 6pm – 11pm*

3 🔊 1.21 Listen to Bryan and Lynn talking about the restaurants. Which one do they choose? Why?

4 Read the restaurant menu. Which dishes would you like to try? Look on R-5 to check any words you don't know.

Bryan and Lynn are cousins. They want to celebrate Lynn's birthday.

STARTERS
Soup of the day
Pear, apple and cheese salad (v)
Warm olives with oil and bread (v)

MAIN COURSES
Home-made pasta in a tomato and olive sauce (v)
Grilled salmon with potatoes and green salad
Steak in a mushroom sauce with roasted potatoes
Fried rice with mushrooms (v)
Prawns and green vegetables with a fresh cucumber salad

DESSERTS
Warm chocolate cake - with chocolate or vanilla ice cream (v)
Cheese plate with toast (v)
Fresh fruit salad with cream (v)

(v) – suitable for vegetarians

5 🔊 1.22 Listen to Lynn and Bryan ordering their meals. Tick (✓) the things they order.

VOCABULARY
Ordering a meal

6 a Put the lines of the restaurant conversation in order, 1–12.

Waiter
- ☐5 OK. And for you, sir?
- ☐1 Hi, are you ready to order?
- ☐ All right. Can I get you something to drink?
- ☐ Fine, and how would you like your steak?
- ☐ Today it's cream of mushroom soup.
- ☐ Sure. Sparkling or still?

Customers
- ☐ Can we have a bottle of water?
- ☐ Could I have the cheese salad to start ... and then the steak?
- ☐ OK, so I'll have that and the pasta, please.
- ☐ Medium, please.
- ☐ Still, please.
- ☐2 Yes, I think so. What's the soup of the day?

b 🔊1.22 Listen again to check.

PRONUNCIATION
Schwa /ə/ sound

7 a 🔊1.23 Words or syllables without stress often have a schwa /ə/ sound. Listen and say the sentence.

Can we have a bottle of water?

b Mark the /ə/ sounds in the rest of the customers' sentences in 6a.

c 🔊1.24 Listen and read the script on R-15 to check. ℗ Practise saying the sentences.

SPEAKING

8 a Look at the menu and decide what you want to order.

b Work in groups of three. Student A, you're the waiter. Students B and C, you're the customers. Order a meal.

c Have two more conversations. Take turns to be the waiter.

Describing a meal

GRAMMAR
Nouns with prepositional phrases

1 Look at sentences 1 and 2. Then circle the nouns and underline the prepositional phrases in 3–6.

1. Soup of the day
2. Warm chocolate cake with ice cream
3. Fresh fruit salad with ice cream
4. Pasta in a tomato and olive sauce
5. Warm olives with oil and bread
6. Steak in a mushroom sauce with roasted potatoes

2 a Put the highlighted phrase in the correct place in each sentence.

1. I'd like to book a table, please. for two
2. My parents cook a big meal every weekend. for nine or ten people
3. Could I have the chicken, please? in garlic sauce
4. That table is free. Why don't we sit there? in the corner
5. Would you like a bottle with your meal? of water
6. The weather was great, so we sat at a table. on the terrace
7. There's a good menu and the staff are very friendly. with lots of vegetarian dishes
8. I'll have the salmon, please. with rice

Grammar reference and practice, R-8

b 🔊1.25 Listen to check. ℗

SPEAKING

3 a Think about a meal you had recently.

1. Where did you have the meal: in a restaurant or café?   at a party?   at a friend's house?
2. When did you have it? Who with?
3. What did you eat? How was the food?
4. What was the place like?
5. Did you have a good time?

> We went to Abla's. It's a Lebanese restaurant with really friendly staff. We sat at a table in the corner ...

b In groups, describe your meals. Give details.

Target activity

Plan a meal

Manuel from Chile

Susanne from Germany

Sarah from South Africa

Eren from Turkey

TASK LISTENING

1 🔊 1.26 Four people are planning a barbecue, but some of their friends are vegetarian. What do they decide to do? Listen and choose from 1–4.

1 cook meat and vegetables together
2 cook only meat but make some salads too
3 cook meat and vegetables on different grills
4 cook only vegetables

2 🔊 1.27 Listen to the second part of the conversation. Tick (✓) the things they need for the salad.

lettuce   black olives   parmesan cheese   olive oil
feta cheese   limes   garlic   tomatoes

TASK VOCABULARY

Making suggestions

3 a Can you remember which six of these suggestions the friends make?

1 How about we organise a barbecue?
2 We could do some pasta.
3 We can put veggies on the barbecue as well.
4 Why don't we get some burgers?
5 Sausages are nice.
6 How about a fruit salad?
7 Perhaps we should make a cake.
8 What about fruit?
9 Melons?

b 🔊 1.26 🔊 1.27 Listen again to check.

TASK

4 a You're going to plan a meal for your group. Work alone and think about these questions.

1 Should you eat inside or outside? Could the meal be in or near your home?
2 What kind of food should you make? How many courses? What about drinks?
3 Who should make the food? How can you help?

b Now think about how to:

1 describe the food.   *Chicken with ...*
2 give opinions.   *I think we should ...*
3 make suggestions.   *How about ... ?*

5 In groups, plan your meal. Make a list of the dishes you decide to make.

6 Read the other groups' lists. Which meals do you think sound the nicest or the most interesting?

Keyword *with*

1 a Match 1–3 with a–c to make three sentences.

1 I've never been very good
2 I work
3 It has a good menu

a with lots of vegetarian dishes. Unit 3
b with the sales team. Unit 2
c with computers. Unit 2

b Which sentence has: a noun + with?   an adjective + with?   a verb + with?

2 Choose the best endings for 1–9.

1 I have an appointment with
2 I've got a problem with
3 I had a meeting with
4 I'm bored with
5 What's wrong with
6 My new flat's nice but I'm not very happy with
7 I'm staying with
8 Steve's going out with
9 The tour of the castle starts with

a Cecile? She looks ill.
b the view.
c a walk around its famous gardens.
d my computer. It won't start up.
e this film. Can we change channels?
f Erika now. They met at a party a month ago.
g the sales team yesterday.
h friends in Honolulu right now. It's wonderful here.
i Dr Jones for two o'clock.

3 a Complete five or six of these sentences with your own ideas.

I'm (not very) good with ...   I work with ...   I have a meeting with ...   I've got a problem with ...
I'm bored with ...   I'm (not very) happy with ...   I sometimes stay with ...   My day usually starts with ...

b Compare your ideas in groups. Ask questions to find out more.

> Well, at the moment I've got a problem with my car.

> OK. What's wrong with it?

Across cultures Mealtimes

1 🔊 1.28 Listen to Matt and Carlos talking about mealtimes. Who talks about these things?

breakfast   the evening meal   dinner on Friday evenings   dinner with guests

2 Can you remember who said these things, Matt or Carlos? 🔊 1.28 Listen again to check.

1 We usually eat together in the evening.
2 Everyone sits around the table and eats and talks.
3 In my family, we all have breakfast at different times.
4 I send my kids to wash their hands before dinner.
5 My mum says *bon appétit* before we start eating.
6 We usually have a quick meal in front of the TV.

3 a Talk together.

1 What time do you usually have meals? Are meals quick or do they take a long time?
2 Do you eat at the same time as other people? Do you eat in the same room?
3 Do you say or do anything before you begin a meal?
4 What do you do while you're eating? (talk? watch TV? smoke? something else?)
5 If you talk, what do you usually talk about?
6 Where you live, do you think food and mealtimes are a very important part of:
   a family life?   b social life?   c work or business life?

b Now think about these questions and talk again.

1 Are the things in 3a the same or different in other places you know?
2 Have you ever had a meal in someone's home in another country? What was it like?

Matt

Carlos

1 **a** Look at the pictures of two snacks and items A–H. Which items do you think you need for bruschetta and which for spiced nuts?

Warm spiced nuts

b Read the recipe for bruschetta to check.

Tomato and cheese bruschetta

Tomato and cheese bruschetta

2 medium tomatoes, chopped
100g mozzarella cheese, chopped
2–3 basil leaves
40 ml extra virgin olive oil
salt, pepper
4 slices of good white bread
1 clove of garlic, peeled

Chop the tomatoes and mozzarella and put them in a bowl. Add the basil, oil, salt and pepper. Stir, then leave for 20 minutes to an hour. Toast the bread until golden brown, then put on a plate. Cut the garlic clove in half and rub over each piece of toast. Put a quarter of the tomato mixture on each slice and serve.

2 **a** Which of these verbs can you find in the recipe for bruschetta?

chop   cut   pour   shake   serve   stir

You can look up the words on R-5.

b In pairs, take turns to mime and guess the verbs for preparing.

3 What kinds of foods do you cook in these ways? Talk together.

bake   boil   fry   grill   roast   toast

Look on R-5 to check any words you don't know.

> I sometimes bake cakes.
>> I never bake bread!

4 Read the recipe for warm spiced nuts. Choose the correct verbs.

Warm spiced nuts

200g mixed nuts
40ml olive oil
a little salt
10ml chopped fresh rosemary
5ml chopped dried chillies

Put the nuts, oil and salt in a bowl. [1] Chop / Shake the fresh rosemary and dried chillies and add to the bowl. [2] Cut / Stir all the ingredients, then pour onto a baking tray. [3] Bake / Boil at 180°C for 15 to 20 minutes, shaking once. [4] Pour / Stir the nuts onto kitchen paper and then into a dish. [5] Shake / Serve warm.

5 Read both recipes again.

1 Which snack do you think is the easiest to make?
2 Would you like to try these snacks? Why? / Why not?

6 **a** Think of a snack or some other quick dish that you know how to make.

b Write the ingredients for your recipe.

c Write the instructions for your recipe.

7 Look at each other's recipes. Ask and answer the questions.

1 Would you like to try them?
2 Can you understand all the instructions?

3 Look again ♻

Review

VOCABULARY Opinions

1 a Put the words in order to make sentences.

1 are better than fresh ones frozen vegetables I think .
2 seven days a week should open shops I don't think .
3 should buy everyone If you ask me, local food .
4 expensive restaurants I find quite stressful .
5 ready-made meals very good for you I don't think are .

b Talk about the opinions. Do you agree with them?

VOCABULARY Ordering a meal

2 a As a class make a café menu. Suggest your favourite dishes. Include:

starters   main dishes   desserts   drinks

Then think about what you'd like to order.

b Work in groups of three: one waiter, two customers. Order a meal. Take turns to be the waiter.

> Hi, are you ready to order?
>> Yes, I'd like the bruschetta, please.

CAN YOU REMEMBER? Unit 2 – Studying, Working conditions

3 a Work in two teams, A and B.

A, how many expressions about studying can you remember?
Make a list: *IT skills, do a degree ...*
B, how many expressions about working conditions can you remember?
Make a list: *pay, working hours ...*

b Look back at unit 2 to check.
A, look on p19. B, look on p21.

c Follow the instructions for the quiz.

1 Choose five expressions to test the other teams.
2 Write sentences with gaps.
3 Take turns to read your sentences to the other teams.
4 Guess the words. You win a point for every correct word, and a bonus point if you can spell it.

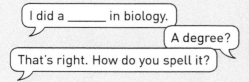

> I did a _____ in biology.
>> A degree?
> That's right. How do you spell it?

Extension

SPELLING AND SOUNDS *oi, oy*

4 a 🔊 1.29 You say oi and oy in the same way: /ɔɪ/. Listen, then say the words.

enjoy   employee   noisy   boil

b Complete the rules with oi or oy.

1 We usually write _____ before a consonant.
2 We usually write _____ before a vowel or at the end of a word.

c 🔊 1.30 Spellcheck. Listen to eight words and write them down.

d Look at the script on R-16 to check your spelling.

NOTICE Making sentences stronger / weaker

5 a Look at these sentences from Judi Bevan's article, *In Defence of Supermarkets*. Decide where the missing words go in each sentence. Then look back at the article on p27 to check.

1 I can find ↓ the ingredients I need at my local supermarket.   all
2 ... vegetables from every continent are a few minutes away.   only
3 In some stores I can shop 24 hours.   even
4 The food was not good ...   always
5 ... there was no choice,   almost
6 ... and the shopkeepers were not friendly.   very
7 And at that time, food was expensive.   very
8 But it's much better than what we had before.   much

b Cover the highlighted words. Can you remember the complete sentences 1–8?

Self-assessment

Can you do these things in English? Circle a number on each line. 1 = I can't do this, 5 = I can do this well.

◉ give opinions	1	2	3	4	5
◉ talk about food and eating	1	2	3	4	5
◉ order a meal in a restaurant	1	2	3	4	5
◉ make suggestions	1	2	3	4	5
◉ give and understand written instructions	1	2	3	4	5

• For Wordcards, reference and saving your work » e-Portfolio
• For more practice » Self-study Pack, Unit 3

4 Encounters

Taxi!

4.1 goals
@ use a taxi

VOCABULARY
Taxis

1 **Ask and answer the questions together.**

1. How often do you use taxis in your own city? What do you use them for?
2. What about when you're travelling?
3. When was your last trip by taxi? Where did you go?

2 a **Read the questions. Match the highlighted expressions with A–F in the pictures.**

1. When was the last time you phoned for a taxi or got a taxi at a taxi rank?
2. How much is the minimum fare for a taxi in your city?
3. What's the maximum number of passengers a taxi can usually take?
4. Do taxis in your city always use a meter? What about in other cities you know?
5. Do you usually ask the driver to keep the change?
6. Do you ever ask for a receipt at the end of a journey?

b 🎧 1.31 Listen to check. ℗

SPEAKING

3 **Ask and answer the questions together. Find out more.**

> The last time I got a taxi at a taxi rank was two weeks ago.

> Really? Where was that?

> It was outside the train station. It was raining and ...

34

Two journeys

LISTENING

Tony is a taxi driver in Vancouver, Canada.

1 **1.32** Listen to Tony's conversations with two passengers, first Nicola and then Dan.

1 Who wants to go to:
   a a bank?   b a hotel?   c the airport?
2 Who asks Tony:
   a for a receipt?   b to wait?   c how much the journey will cost?

2 a Can you remember if these sentences are true or false?

1 It's Nicola's first time in Canada.
2 She wants to go to a hotel.
3 Dan goes to the bank to get some money.
4 He's going on a business trip.
5 It costs more than $30 from the bank to the airport.

b **1.32** Listen again to check.

3 Do you ever chat with people you meet in these situations? What do you talk about?

in a taxi   on a plane / bus / train   waiting for a bus   sharing a table in a café

VOCABULARY
Getting a taxi

4 a Match what the passengers say 1–8 with the driver's replies a–h.

The start of a journey

1 How much is it to the city centre?
2 Can you take me to the Park Inn?
3 I'd like to go to the airport, please.
4 Can I put my case in the back?

a The Park Inn on Broadway, right?
b I'll do that for you.
c It's usually about thirty, thirty-five dollars.
d OK. Which terminal?

The end of a journey

5 Could you wait here for five minutes?
6 How much is it?
7 Just make it thirty-five dollars.
8 And can I have a receipt, please?

e Thanks very much ... And here's your change, fifteen dollars.
f Well, OK, but can you pay me first?
g Sure ... Here you are.
h Thirty-one fifty, please.

b Cover 1–8 and look at a–h. Can you remember what the passengers say?

PRONUNCIATION
Sentence stress and schwa /ə/

5 a Mark the stressed syllables in these sentences.

1 How much is it to the city centre?
2 Can you take me to the Park Inn?
3 I'd like to go to the airport, please.
4 Can I put my case in the back?
5 And can I have a receipt, please?

b Remember that words or syllables without stress often have a schwa /ə/ sound. Mark the /ə/ sounds in the sentences in 5a.

1 How much is it to the city centre?

c **1.33** Listen and read the script on R-16 to check. ℗ Practise saying the sentences.

SPEAKING

6 a You're going to take a taxi. Work alone and think about these questions.

1 Where are you?
2 Where do you want to go?
3 What's the reason for your journey?
4 What will you chat about with the driver? (the weather, the traffic, your job ...)

How much is it to Broad Street?

Usually about six dollars.

OK. Can you take me to the OSP building, please?

b Take turns to be the passenger and taxi driver. Have conversations with three parts:

the start of your journey   →   a short chat   →   the end of your journey

c Change pairs and have two more conversations.

Hack

4.2 goals
- describe past events
- tell a story

Melissa Plaut is one of only 400 women among New York's 40,000 taxi drivers. "I started driving a cab after losing my boring office job," says Melissa. "I didn't want to work in an office again, so I decided to get my cab licence." She started a blog about her experiences as a taxi driver, newyorkhack. blogspot.com, which quickly became popular. She's also written a book called *Hack*. In New York, hack is slang for taxi, or taxi driver.

READING

1 Read the information about Melissa Plaut, a New York taxi driver.

1 How did Melissa become a taxi driver?
2 Where can you read about her experiences as a driver?

2 a You're going to read a true story from Melissa's blog. Look at these words and expressions from the story and guess what happened.

a Canadian man   the airport   a wallet   credit card
phoned   shopping   fifty dollars   laughed

b Read the story to check your ideas.

---

www.newyorkhack.blogspot.com

During rush hour, a Canadian man and his teenage son got in the cab and asked me to take them to La Guardia airport. They were going back to Canada. We had a nice conversation together and when they got out, they gave me a good tip.

When my next passenger got in, he handed me a wallet and said he found it on the back seat. I immediately knew it belonged to the Canadian man. It contained a driving license and a credit card, nothing much else.

Now, I liked the Canadian guy, so I found the 800 number on the back of the credit card and phoned the company. I explained what happened and gave them my number. After about half an hour, the Canadian guy called and asked me to go back to the airport and return the wallet. So I turned off my cab light and I started for the airport. Five or six people tried to stop me as I was driving through the city, but I didn't stop. I was doing a good thing!

Forty minutes later, I arrived at La Guardia. The guy was standing outside the terminal building and looking pretty stressed. I gave back the wallet and told him that I only did a little shopping with his credit card! Just a joke. He was so happy, he just laughed. "You're my favourite New Yorker ever," he said. Then he handed me fifty dollars and ran back into the airport. The whole thing – plus the fifty dollars! – really made my night.

---

3 Read the story again. Answer the questions in groups.

1 Why do you think Melissa liked the Canadian man?
2 How did the Canadian man know Melissa's phone number?
3 Why do you think the Canadian man was looking stressed when Melissa saw him?
4 Why did the Canadian man laugh?
5 How did Melissa feel at the end of the story? Why, do you think?

4 What do you think are the good and bad points about being a taxi driver? Talk together.

Telling a story

1 a Cover the blog. Use the words in the box to complete the sentences from the story.

1 _____ rush hour, a Canadian man and his teenage son got in the cab and ...
2 _____ my next passenger got in, he handed me a wallet and ...
3 _____ about half an hour, the Canadian guy called and ...
4 Five or six people tried to stop me _____ I was driving through the city, but ...
5 Forty minutes _____, I arrived at La Guardia. The guy was ...
6 "You're my favourite New Yorker ever," he said. _____ he handed me fifty dollars and ...

b Look at the story again to check.

2 Cover the story. In pairs, tell the whole story using the sentences in 1a for help.

3 a Look at the beginning of Melissa's story. Then choose a or b.

> past simple
>
> ... a Canadian man and his teenage son got in the cab and asked me to take them to La Guardia airport. They were going back to Canada.
>
> past progressive

When Melissa met the Canadian man and his son:
a their journey to Canada was finished.
b they were in the middle of their journey to Canada.

b Circle the correct words.

1 Use the past simple / progressive to talk about a finished action.
2 Use the past simple / progressive to say an action was in progress in the past.

4 a Complete the sentences with was, were, wasn't, weren't.

was / were + -ing	
❓ What _____ he doing?	❓ _____ they going back to Canada?
➕ He was standing outside the terminal.	✅ Yes, they were.
➖ He _____ looking very happy.	❌ No, they _____.

b 🔊 1.34 Listen to check. Ⓟ Do we say was and were with a schwa /ə/ in:

a questions and positive sentences, or
b negative sentences and short answers?

5 a Look at three pictures from the start of a story. Use the best form, the past simple or the past progressive, to complete the paragraph.

The Ten-Dollar Bill

One sunny morning a man [1]_____ (walk) through the city on his way to work. He [2]_____ (wear) a smart suit and tie and [3]_____ (talk) on his phone. Suddenly, the sun [4]_____ (go) in and it [5]_____ (start) raining heavily. The man [6]_____ (see) a taxi and [7]_____ (start) running towards it. As he [8]_____ (run), a $10 bill [9]_____ (fall) from his pocket onto the ground, but he didn't notice. He [10]_____ (get) into the cab, [11]_____ (shut) the door, and the cab [12]_____ (drive) away.

b 🔊 1.35 Listen to check. Ⓟ

6 a In pairs, look at the pictures from the rest of the story on R-2. Plan how to tell the rest of the story. Think about how to do these things.

• describe the events in the story • link the events together
• describe people, places and the weather • add extra information

b Practise telling your story together.

7 Listen to each other's stories. What are the differences between them?

Tell stories about memorable meetings

4.3 goals
- describe past events ♻
- tell a travel anecdote

Osman   Bernd

Annie   Lukas

TASK LISTENING

1 **a** The people in the pictures have just met each other. Where are they? Do you think they're having a good time together?

b ▶ 1.36 Listen to Osman's and Annie's stories. Check your ideas.

2 **a** Which sentence in each pair is about Osman and Bernd? Which is about Annie and Lukas?

1	a They met in Germany.	b They met in France.
2	a They were going to the US on business.	b They had French lessons together.
3	a They met one or two years ago.	b They met a long time ago.
4	a They met a few times.	b They only met once.
5	a They're not in contact now.	b Now they're pen friends.

b ▶ 1.36 Listen again to check.

TASK VOCABULARY

Starting a story

3 **a** Make sentences for starting a story.

1	I was	a	for a little restaurant.	6	I was	f	for a train.
2	I was living	b	in France.	7	It was	g	in a shop.
3	I was looking	c	in Frankfurt.	8	I was working	h	summer.
4	I was on my way	d	my brother.	9	I was travelling	i	to the USA.
5	I was visiting	e	to a conference.	10	I was waiting	j	with two friends.

b Look at 1–10 again. Think of more ways to complete each sentence.

TASK

4 **a** Think of a time in your life when you met someone interesting. Think about these questions.

1 Where were you? When was it?
2 What were you doing?
3 What was the person like?
4 What did you talk about?
5 Did you spend much time together?
6 Are you in contact now?

b Tell each other about the people you met.

Keyword *back*

verbs with *back*

1 a Read the sentences. How do the two highlighted expressions differ in meaning?

> a I'd like to go to the airport, please. Unit 4
> b The Canadian guy called and asked me to go back to the airport. Unit 4

b Add *back* to the correct place in each sentence.

> 1 Could you wait? I'll be in five minutes. Unit 4
> 2 … a Canadian man and his son were going to Canada. Unit 4
> 3 I gave the wallet and told him I only did a *little* shopping! Unit 4
> 4 He handed me fifty dollars and ran into the airport. Unit 4

back (opposite of *front*)

2 Which highlighted expressions refer to:

a a motorbike?   b a car?   c a credit card?

> 1 Can I put my case in the back? Unit 4
> 2 He handed me a wallet and said he found it on the back seat. Unit 4
> 3 I found the number on the back and phoned the company. Unit 4
> 4 I really wanted to ride it, not sit on the back! Unit 1

3 a Complete the questions with the words and expressions in the box.

> a shop   car   home   how quickly   old ~~the next day~~   travelled   wardrobe

1 Have you ever flown to a different country and come back *the next day*?
2 Have you ever been back to your _____ school or college?
3 When someone texts you, _____ do you text them back? What about emails?
4 When was the last time you took something back to _____? What was it?
5 What's the first thing you do when you get back _____ after a day at work or college?
6 Do you know anyone who's _____ on the back of an elephant?
7 Have you ever spent the night on the back seat of a _____?
8 What things do you keep in the back of your _____?

b Ask and answer the questions together.

> Well, a few months ago I took a pair of jeans back to a shop.   Oh. Why?

Independent learning English outside the classroom

Astrid from Mexico

Tom from England

Masha from Russia

1 a 🔊 1.37 Listen to three people talking about how they learn languages outside the classroom. Which things A–E does each person talk about?

b 🔊 1.37 How do they use the things in the pictures? Listen again and make notes.

Astrid – read children's books

c What do you think about their ideas? Why? Talk together.

2 a Can you think of more ways of learning English outside the classroom? Make a list of your ideas. Think about listening, speaking, reading and writing.

b Compare with the list on R-2.

3 Talk together. Which of the ideas for learning outside the classroom:

1 do you do now?   2 do you like / not like?   3 would you like to try?

Tony

Valérie

1 a 🔊 1.38 **Listen to a conversation between Tony and Valérie.**

1 Why's Valérie in Vancouver?
2 What does she do?

b Do you think they have a friendly conversation? Why? / Why not?

2 Read the conversation.

1 How many questions does Tony ask?
2 Which **highlighted** expressions in the text are used:
   a to show interest? *So ...*
   b to add extra information? *Actually, ...*
3 <u>Underline</u> the extra information Valérie gives in her answers.

3 a In pairs, write the next five lines of Valérie and Tony's conversation.

b Compare your conversations with another pair. Were your ideas the same or different?

4 a Think of four questions for starting a conversation. Use the expressions in A below or your own ideas.

b In A/B pairs, use your questions to start conversations. Then continue the conversations.

A	Are you interested in ... ?	Do you like ... ?
	What's your favourite ... ?	Have you seen ... ?
	Have you ever been to ... ?	Where do you ... ?
	Are you going to ... ?	Have you got ... ?

↓

B	Answer the question. Give some extra information.

↓   ↑

A	Listen carefully to what your partner says. Ask another question.

5 Tell another partner about the conversations you had.

1 What did you talk about?
2 What was your most interesting conversation?

VALÉRIE	Good morning, can you take me to the Holiday Inn, please?
TONY	Sure. Which one?
VALÉRIE	The one on Broadway, please.
TONY	So, what brings you to Vancouver?
VALÉRIE	I have some old friends here. Actually, <u>we were at university together</u>.
TONY	So it's not your first time here?
VALÉRIE	Oh, no. I visit every three or four months.
TONY	Right. So you like it here?
VALÉRIE	Yes. In fact, I'd really like to live here.
TONY	Oh, yeah? Where do you live?
VALÉRIE	In Montreal. Well, actually, I've got a small business there.
TONY	Really? What do you do?
VALÉRIE	I own a couple of restaurants.

Do you like football?

Yes. Actually, I play for a team at work.

So where do you play?

4 Look again ♻

Review

VOCABULARY Getting a taxi

1 a Put the words in 1–8 in the correct order.

1 is centre much it city How the to ?
2 you Can the take Park Inn to me ?
3 like to station to the please I'd go .
4 suitcases the I my put in Can back ?
5 five Could for minutes here you wait ?
6 it much is How ?
7 Just thirty it make dollars .
8 Can a have receipt I please ?

b In pairs, take turns to say 1–8 and think of answers.

GRAMMAR The past progressive

2 a Choose a time from yesterday. Make sure you all choose a different time.

b Find out what different people were doing at the time you chose. Make notes.

> What were you doing at 9.30 in the evening?
>
> Hm ... I think I was having a shower.

c Choose one of the people in your class. Make sure you all choose a different person.

d Find out from the others what your person did yesterday. Make notes.

> What can you tell me about Jakub?
>
> Well, at 9.30 pm he was having a shower.

e In groups, tell each other what your people did yesterday. Who had the most interesting day?

> In the morning, Jakub drove to work. He had a meeting and ...

CAN YOU REMEMBER? Unit 3 – Ordering a meal

3 a Complete the restaurant conversation.

WAITER   Hi, are you ¹_____ to order?
CUSTOMER   Yes. What's the soup of the ²_____?
WAITER   It's vegetable soup ³_____ fresh herbs.
CUSTOMER   That sounds nice. I'll ⁴_____ that and the fish, please.
WAITER   All right. And for you, sir?
CUSTOMER   ⁵_____ I have the green salad to start and then the steak?
WAITER   Yes, and ⁶_____ would you like your steak?
CUSTOMER   ⁷_____, please.
WAITER   And can I ⁸_____ you something to drink?
CUSTOMER   Can we have a bottle ⁹_____ water, please?
WAITER   Of course. ¹⁰_____ or still?
CUSTOMER   Still, please.
WAITER   OK, thanks very much.

b Practise in groups of three. Change the food and drink to make new conversations.

Extension

SPELLING AND SOUNDS gh

4 a 🔊 1.39 gh is usually silent. Listen, then say the words.

right   night   frightening   eight   neighbours   bought   through   straight

b 🔊 1.40 In a few words, gh is pronounced /f/ or /g/. Listen, then say the words.

/f/   enough   laugh
/g/   yoghurt   spaghetti

c 🔊 1.41 Spellcheck. Close your book. Listen to ten words with gh and write them down.

d Look at the script on R-17 to check your spelling.

NOTICE find

5 a Look at the sentences from this unit. Which highlighted expression describes a feeling or an opinion? Which describe an action?

1 ... when my next passenger got in, he handed me a wallet and said he found it on the back seat.
2 I liked the Canadian guy, so I found the number on the back of the credit card and phoned the company.
3 When I was learning French ... I liked reading children's books. I found it very useful because the sentences are very simple.

b Ask and answer the questions in groups.

1 Have you ever found something on the street, in a taxi, etc.? What was it? What did you do?
2 What was the last thing you lost? Did you ever find it?
3 What situations or things do you find: stressful? boring? fascinating? terrifying? funny? inconvenient?

> I find travelling stressful.
>
> Why? I usually find it really interesting.

Self-assessment

Can you do these things in English? Circle a number on each line. 1 = I can't do this, 5 = I can do this well.

◉ use a taxi	1	2	3	4	5
◉ tell a story	1	2	3	4	5
◉ tell a travel anecdote	1	2	3	4	5
◉ describe past events	1	2	3	4	5
◉ show interest in a conversation	1	2	3	4	5
◉ develop a conversation by asking questions and giving longer answers	1	2	3	4	5

- For Wordcards, reference and saving your work » e-Portfolio
- For more practice » Self-study Pack, Unit 4

5 Money

5.1 goals
- change money
- understand instructions on a cash machine
- pay for things in different places

Money matters

VOCABULARY
Money

1 a Read the questions. Match the highlighted words and expressions with the things in pictures A–F.

1 How many different coins and notes are there in your country? What pictures do they have on them?
2 How often do you use a cash machine or go into a bank? What do you do at each place?
3 When you go shopping, how do you prefer to pay? (in cash? by card? another way?)
4 How do you usually pay bills? Do you ever use the Internet for paying bills, banking or shopping?

b 🔊 2.1 Listen to check. 🅟

2 Ask and answer the questions together.

LISTENING

3 🔊 2.2 Thiago's flying from France to Scotland. Before his flight, he changes some money in the airport. Listen to Thiago's conversation.

1 How much money does he change?
2 How much does he get?

4 a Match the questions and answers. Which questions does Thiago ask? Which does the assistant ask?

1 Do you have Scottish pounds?
2 Can I change these euros, please?
3 That's a hundred and eighty euros, yes?
4 Sorry, do you have any smaller notes?

a No problem. Are twenties OK?
b Of course.
c No, we don't.
d Yes, that's right.

b 🔊 2.2 Listen again to check.

SPEAKING

5 a How many different currencies can you think of? *euros, pounds ...*

b You're going to change money at a bureau de change. Decide:
- which currency you want to change, and how much
- which currency you want to get

c Have conversations in different pairs. Take turns to be the customer and assistant.

READING

6 Thiago uses a cash machine in Glasgow, Scotland. Put the screens A–E on p43 in order. Then answer the questions.

1 Which buttons on screen A, 1–6, can you press if you want to:
a get some money?
b change your PIN number?
c know how much money you have?
2 Find words or expressions in screens A–E that mean:
a choose　　b question　　c how much

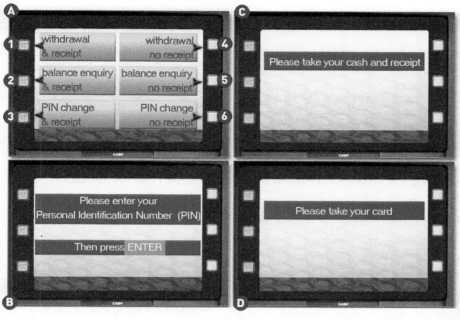

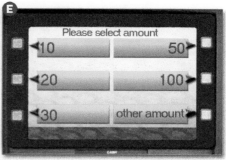

How would you like to pay?

LISTENING

1 **2.3** Listen to three conversations with Thiago in Glasgow. In each conversation:

a Where is he?
1 a bus station 3 a shop
2 a museum 4 a restaurant
b Does he pay in cash or by card?

2 **2.3** Listen again and complete the information.

Conversation 1 Thiago buys some _____ They cost _____
The assistant asks him if he'd like a _____
Conversation 2 The waitress asks Thiago to type in his PIN and press _____
She gives him a _____
Conversation 3 The receptionist asks to see a _____ His ticket costs _____
He pays with a £ _____ note.

VOCABULARY
Paying for things

3 **a** Which of these questions does Thiago ask?

1 Anything else?
2 How much‿is that?
3 Can‿I pay by card?
4 Would you like‿a bag?
5 Could‿I have the bill?
6 How would you like to pay?
7 Do you take cards?
8 Can‿I see your student card?
9 Do you have‿anything smaller?

b Think of ways to answer all the questions. Then compare your ideas with the script on R-17.

PRONUNCIATION
Linking consonants and vowels 1

4 **2.4** Listen to questions 1–9. Notice how consonant and vowel sounds link (‿). Does a consonant or a vowel come:

1 at the end of the first word? 2 at the start of the next word?

5 In pairs, practise asking the questions and giving different answers. **P**

SPEAKING

6 **a** Work in A/B pairs.

A, look at your role cards on R-2.
B, look at your role cards on R-4.

Hello, can I help you?
Yes, do you have …

b Have two conversations.

Microcredit

READING

1 **Why do people borrow money from banks? Make a list of reasons.**

to buy a home ...

2 **Complete the sentences with these words.**

| credit   interest   a loan   repayments |

1 I borrowed some money from the bank. → I got _____ / _____ from the bank.
2 Now I pay money to the bank every month. → I make _____ every month.
3 Borrowing the money costs seven percent a year. → I pay seven percent _____ a year.

3 **a** **What do you think *microcredit* is? Is it credit for:**

1 people without much money?
2 buying computer software?
3 the education of children?

b **Read the article to check.**

A new kind of banking?

✦ In 1976, Muhammed Yunus, a Bangladeshi professor of economics, started Grameen Bank. Grameen gives small loans – usually no more than US$100 – to very poor people who can't get credit from normal banks. This kind of credit is called *microcredit.*

✦ Most of Grameen's customers live in villages in the Bangladeshi countryside. 97 percent of them are women. They use the credit to start small businesses and make money for their families. For example, they make furniture, repair clothes, or buy animals for milk.

✦ Customers usually have to make repayments every week for twelve months. They pay about 16 percent interest a year. Grameen says that 98 percent of its customers make all their repayments.

✦ People who want a loan from Grameen have to make groups of five people, called loan circles. The people in the circle meet regularly to talk about their ideas and help each other. If someone in the group doesn't make their repayments, no one in the group can get credit in the future. However, if everyone makes their repayments, they can get bigger loans.

✦ In 2007, Grameen Bank had over seven million customers in nearly eighty thousand villages. There are now more than seven thousand other microcredit organisations around the world, including in Europe and the United States.

✦ Professor Yunus and Grameen Bank won the Nobel Peace Prize in December 2006.

4 **Read the article again. What are these numbers in the text?**

100   97   12   16   98   5   7,000,000   80,000   7,000

SPEAKING

5 **Talk together.**

1 Why do you think most of Grameen's customers are women?
2 Why do you think Professor Yunus got the Nobel Peace Prize? Do you think he was a good choice?

READING

6 **a** **You're going to find out about two people who used microcredit to start businesses. They make the things in the pictures. What would you like to find out? In pairs, write two questions.**

Where are the people from?

b Try to find the answers to your questions. Student A, read Alice's story on this page. Student B, read Rukmani's story on R-3.

http://www.microcreditsummit.org/stories/alice.htm

BORROWER SUCCESS STORIES
MICROCREDIT SUMMIT CAMPAIGN

When Alice Pallewela got married, she and her husband went to live in Yodagama, a tiny farming village in the west of Sri Lanka.

"My husband works for the government, but his pay isn't enough for both of us," explains Alice. "I needed to make some money, so I decided to sell sweets. I've always loved sweets, and there weren't any sweet shops in Yodagama."

Alice started her business with a loan of US$100. She makes a few different kinds of sweets, all with local ingredients. She now employs six young women, and her sweets have an excellent reputation.

SPEAKING

7 Tell each other about Alice and Rukmani. Whose story do you find the most interesting? Why?

You have to ...

GRAMMAR

have to, can

1 a Look at the grammar table. Circle the correct expressions in sentences 1–4.

have to	can
1 Grameen's customers <u>have to</u> / <u>don't have to</u> make groups of five people. 2 They <u>have to</u> / <u>don't have to</u> be women.	3 They <u>can</u> / <u>can't</u> usually get credit from normal banks. 4 They <u>can</u> / <u>can't</u> get bigger loans if they make all their repayments.
_____ they have to be women? Yes, they _____ . No, they _____ .	_____ they get credit from normal banks? Yes, they _____ . No, they _____ .

b Answer the questions.

1   Which highlighted expression means that something is:
    a possible?   b not possible?   c necessary?   d not necessary?
2   Which highlighted expression has a similar meaning to:
    a *need to*?   b *don't need to*?

c Complete the questions and short answers in the table with can, can't, do, don't.

2 🎧 2.5 Listen to sentences 1–4. Notice how we say can /kən/ and to /tə/ with a schwa /ə/. 🅟

3 Work alone. Change these sentences so they're true for your country.

1   You can't get married until you're 21.
2   You can't drink alcohol.
3   Everyone over 18 has to vote.
4   You don't have to serve in the army.
5   You have to go to school until you're 17.
6   You can drive a car when you're 15.
7   You don't have to carry an ID card.
8   You can smoke when you're 16.

Grammar reference and practice, R-9

SPEAKING

4 Compare your sentences in groups. Then ask and answer the questions.

1   If you're from the same country, do you agree?
2   Are there any laws you'd like to change? Why? How would you change them?
3   What do you know about laws in other countries?

I've heard that in the US, you can drive when you're fourteen.

Yes, but not everywhere.

Give advice to a visitor

TASK LISTENING

1 a Look at the pictures and read the situations. Which things, 1–6, do you think you should do? Which things shouldn't you do?

Visiting a home in Canada
1 before the visit, ask if you can bring something
2 take a gift to the hosts
3 wear shoes in their home

Having a hot spring bath in Japan
4 wash yourself before you get into the water
5 get out of the water from time to time and rest
6 make a lot of noise

b 2.6 Listen to Megan and Yukio and check your ideas. Do you find any of the rules surprising?

TASK VOCABULARY

Giving advice

2 What advice did Megan and Yukio give? Match 1–7 with a–g.

Megan from Canada

Yukio from Japan

1 You should probably ask ahead of time
2 Maybe you can bring a
3 Don't wear
4 You have to wash
5 After that, you can get into
6 The water's quite hot, so you shouldn't stay in it
7 You can't make

a your shoes inside.
b if you can bring something with you.
c too long.
d off all the soap, so you are really clean.
e a lot of noise.
f the hot spring.
g bottle of wine, or maybe some flowers, something like that.

TASK

3 a Choose three things that are useful to tell a visitor about your country. Use these or your own ideas.

- visiting a religious building, e.g. a church, a mosque, a temple …
- using a library, public transport, ski slopes, …
- going to a wedding, someone's house for dinner, a restaurant, …

b You're going to tell someone about the three things. Think about the advice you want to give.

You have to …   You can't …   You should probably …   Don't …

> When you go to a mosque, there are a few rules. You have to …

c Listen to each other's advice and ask questions to find out more. If you're from the same country, do you agree?

Keyword *it*

Three uses of *it*

1 a Read the information and answer the questions.

You can use it to talk about:

A things, places and ideas you've mentioned already.

> The water's quite hot so you shouldn't stay in it too long.

B times and dates.

> It was July and I was looking forward to my holiday.

C the weather and temperature.

> It was really nice weather so you could eat outside.

1 What does it refer to in sentence A?
2 Can you think of five more expressions to replace the underlined words?
  a times and dates: It was 1998. *my birthday*
  b the weather: It was rainy. *hot and sunny*

b You're going to talk about an important day from your life. Think about these questions.

When was it? What happened? Why was it important? What was the weather like? How did you feel?

c Tell each other about your important days. Ask questions to find out more.

> It was a summer day in 2005. It was important because it was the day I got married!

Expressions with *it*

2 a Complete the conversations with expressions from the box. **2.7** Then listen to check. ℗

> Don't worry about it   I'll think about it
> It depends   ~~It doesn't really matter~~
> It's up to you   That's it

1 **A** When can we meet? Tomorrow? Sunday?
  B *It doesn't really matter* . I'm free all weekend.
2 **A** I'm sorry I'm late! Where's the meeting?
  B _____. The meeting hasn't started yet.
3 **A** Do you like parties?
  B _____. Generally yes, but not when there are too many people.
4 **A** Do you want to come to the cinema tonight?
  B Mm, I'm not sure I have time. _____, OK?
5 **A** Have we got any food at home?
  B Not really ... we've got some milk in the fridge. _____.
6 **A** What time do I have to start work?
  B _____. But you have to be here eight hours a day.

b Work in pairs. Take turns to start conversations 1–6 and remember the responses.

Across cultures Money

1 Complete the statements with verbs from the box.

> borrow   cost   give   earn   lend   pay (x3)

1 If you need a big loan, you should _____ from your family if you can.
2 If you _____ money to a friend, you shouldn't ask for interest.
3 Parents should _____ some money to their children every week.
4 Adults who live with their parents should _____ rent.
5 You shouldn't talk about how much you _____.
6 You shouldn't ask people how much their home _____.
7 If a man and a woman go to a café, the man should always _____ the bill.
8 If you invite friends to a restaurant, you should _____ for all the food and drink.

2 a **2.8** Listen to Hayley and John. Which statement, 1–8, do they talk about?

b **2.8** Listen again. Who agrees with the statement? Who disagrees with it? Why?

c Read the script on R-18 to check.

3 Think about these questions. Then ask and answer them together.

1 What do you think about statements 1–8? Why?
2 Where you live, what do most people think? Do they have the same ideas as you?
3 What do people think in other regions or countries that you know?

Hayley from the USA
John from the UK

1 a Imagine you're going to visit a friend who lives in another country. What things would you ask your friend about before you go? Make a list.

the weather, clothes ...

b Read Thiago's email to Chris, who lives and works in Cairo. Which things on your list does he ask about?

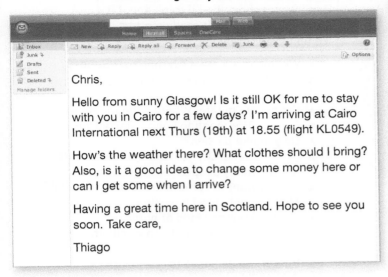

Chris,

Hello from sunny Glasgow! Is it still OK for me to stay with you in Cairo for a few days? I'm arriving at Cairo International next Thurs (19th) at 18.55 (flight KL0549).

How's the weather there? What clothes should I bring? Also, is it a good idea to change some money here or can I get some when I arrive?

Having a great time here in Scotland. Hope to see you soon. Take care,

Thiago

2 Read Chris's reply. Does he answer all Thiago's questions?

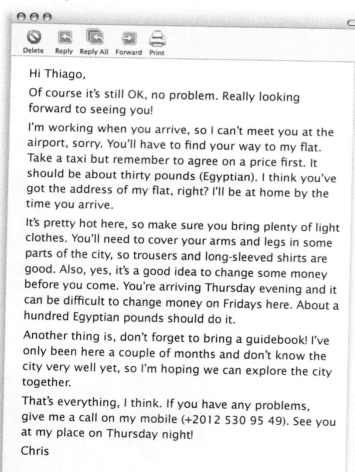

Hi Thiago,

Of course it's still OK, no problem. Really looking forward to seeing you!

I'm working when you arrive, so I can't meet you at the airport, sorry. You'll have to find your way to my flat. Take a taxi but remember to agree on a price first. It should be about thirty pounds (Egyptian). I think you've got the address of my flat, right? I'll be at home by the time you arrive.

It's pretty hot here, so make sure you bring plenty of light clothes. You'll need to cover your arms and legs in some parts of the city, so trousers and long-sleeved shirts are good. Also, yes, it's a good idea to change some money before you come. You're arriving Thursday evening and it can be difficult to change money on Fridays here. About a hundred Egyptian pounds should do it.

Another thing is, don't forget to bring a guidebook! I've only been here a couple of months and don't know the city very well yet, so I'm hoping we can explore the city together.

That's everything, I think. If you have any problems, give me a call on my mobile (+2012 530 95 49). See you at my place on Thursday night!

Chris

Thiago is planning to visit his friend Chris in Cairo.

3 a Cover the emails. Can you remember Thiago's questions and Chris's advice?

Asking for advice
1 What ... should I bring?
2 Is it a good idea to change ... ?

Giving advice
3 You'll have to find your way to ...
4 Remember to agree on ...
5 Make sure you bring plenty of ...
6 You'll need to cover your ...
7 It's a good idea to change ...
8 Don't forget to bring a ...

b Read the emails again to check.

4 Complete the sentences. Use the words in (brackets) and different expressions from 3a.

1 There are lots of insects so ... (buy / insect spray)
2 You can't get into the country without the right visa so ... (get / tourist visa)
3 The museums have discounts for students, so ... (bring / student card)
4 The weather here's freezing, so ... (pack / warm clothes)
5 It's a really long train journey, so ... (bring / good book)

5 a Plan an email or letter to a friend who's going to visit you.

1 Which topics do you want to talk about? Use this list and your own ideas.
   the weather   clothes   money   transport
   where to meet   phone numbers
2 What do you want to say about each topic?
3 How many paragraphs will you write?
4 What will you say in each paragraph?
5 How will you start and finish your email or letter?

b Write your email or letter. Write about 100 words.

6 Read each other's emails or letters. Is there anything else you'd like to know about? Ask questions to find out.

5 Look again ♻

Review

1 a In pairs, decide on the rules for a library. Complete the sentences with: can, can't, have to or don't have to.

1 You _____ pay to join the library.
2 You _____ borrow more than six books.
3 You _____ keep books for up to three weeks.
4 You _____ pay a fine if you keep books too long.
5 You _____ borrow dictionaries.
6 You _____ keep quiet in the library.

b Work alone. Think of the rules and advice for two places. Use can, can't, have to or don't have to.

c In groups, listen to the rules and advice. Can you guess the places?

> Usually you don't have to buy a ticket. You can bring your own food. You shouldn't leave any rubbish ...

> Is it a park?

VOCABULARY Giving advice

2 a Work in pairs. For each situation, think of advice for a friend. Use your own ideas.

1 I'm going on holiday to Paris but I don't speak any French.
2 My manager wants me to work this weekend but friends are coming to stay with me.
3 I promised to meet a friend tonight but I feel too tired now.
4 I really want to stop smoking but I can't.

b Listen to each other's advice. Who has the best ideas?

> We'd tell our friend: You should talk to your manager. Explain that your friends ...

CAN YOU REMEMBER? Unit 4 – Getting a taxi

3 a Match the sentences 1–6 with the responses a–f.

1 How much is it to the city centre?
2 Can you take me to the Park Inn?
3 Could you wait here for five minutes? I just have to get some papers.
4 The Royal Bank on Howe Street, please.
5 Just make it thirty-five dollars.
6 And can I have a receipt, please?

a Sure ... here you are. Have a safe trip now.
b OK.
c Thanks very much ... And here's your change, fifteen dollars.
d The Park Inn on Broadway, right?
e That depends on the traffic.
f Well, OK, but can you pay me first?

b Practise taxi conversations in pairs. Change the underlined parts of the sentences in 3a.

Extension

SPELLING AND SOUNDS -tion, -ssion, -cian

4 a ⏵ 2.9 You say the endings -tion, -ssion, -cian in the same way, /ʃən/. Listen and say the words. Notice how the stress always goes before the ending.

conversation   expression   musician

b Practise saying these words with the correct sound and stress.

politician   station   discussion   reception
electrician   pronunciation

c ⏵ 2.10 Spellcheck. Close your books. Listen to ten words and write them down.

d Look at the script on R-18 to check your spelling.

NOTICE Vague language

5 a What can you remember about the Grameen bank? Complete the sentences with the numbers.

| seven thousand   seven million |
| 16   eighty thousand   100 |

1 Grameen gives small loans – usually no more than US$_____ .
2 They pay about _____ percent interest a year.
3 In 2007, Grameen Bank had over _____ customers in nearly _____ villages.
4 There are now more than _____ other microcredit organisations around the world.

b Look at the article on p44 to check.

c ⏵ 2.11 Listen to eight questions and write down your answers – but don't write them in order. Use the expressions in 5a. *No more than three.*

d Look at each other's answers. Can you guess what they mean? Ask questions to find out more.

> OK, 'No more than three' ... is that how much tea or coffee you drink?

Self-assessment

Can you do these things in English? Circle a number on each line. 1 = I can't do this, 5 = I can do this well.

	1	2	3	4	5
change money	1	2	3	4	5
understand instructions on a cash machine	1	2	3	4	5
pay for things in different places	1	2	3	4	5
talk about rules and obligations	1	2	3	4	5
give advice	1	2	3	4	5
write an email or letter giving advice to a visitor	1	2	3	4	5

• For Wordcards, reference and saving your work ›› e-Portfolio
• For more practice ›› Self-study Pack, Unit 5

Energy

Burning calories

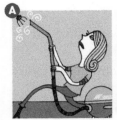     

VOCABULARY
Household chores

1 a What chores can you see in each picture?

> cleaning the windows   doing the cooking   doing the dusting
> doing the ironing   making the bed   doing the vacuuming

b [2.12] Listen to check. ℗ Can you think of more chores?

SPEAKING

2 Talk together.

1 Who does the different chores in your home?
2 Which chores do you like the most? Which don't you like? Why?

3 a Which three chores in 1 do you think use the most energy?

b Read the fact file from a magazine to check your ideas.

Daily chores may do you more good than going to the gym

Doing the vacuuming may be a better way to keep fit than swimming or cycling, according to new research. This is great news for all of us who don't like going to the gym! Here's how some household chores compare to more traditional ways of keeping fit.

	calories an hour
Vacuuming	320
Swimming (20 metres a minute)	270
Walking (5 kilometres per hour)	260
Cycling (10 kilometres per hour)	240
Yoga	230
Ironing	203
Cooking	180
Making beds	180
Cleaning windows	150
Dusting	150

READING

4 a Look at the photos showing two unusual ways to burn calories. What do you think are the advantages of each way?

b Check your ideas in pairs. A, read the article about Manuel Pedro below. B, read the article about Alex Gadsden on R-3.

Manuel Pedro on his treadmill in the office.

Alex Gadsden on his cycle washer outside.

The treadmill

When Manuel Pedro's daughter looked at him one morning and said "Wow, you're fat!", he knew it was time to lose some weight. The trouble was, he didn't have time to do any exercise.

"I work in an office all day and when I get home in the evening, I generally just want to sit down and relax. At the weekend I normally do things with my kids, so I just don't have time to go to the gym or go for a run."

However, one day, his wife suggested buying a treadmill and walking on it while he worked.

"I thought she was crazy at first," he says. "But then I thought, why not?"

So the forty-year-old bought a cheap treadmill and put it in the corner of his office. He fixed his laptop to it and began walking and working at the same time.

"At first, I found it hard to type and walk at the same time. I got really stressed and sometimes only did it once or twice a week. I also looked really stupid in a shirt and tie on a treadmill. My colleagues thought it was really funny."

However, soon Manuel got better at working while he walked, and started to feel healthier. After a while he was doing several hours' walking every morning.

"I have a lot more energy now," says the office manager. "When I get to the office, I get straight on the treadmill and check my emails. I do three hours a day at the moment. Every week I do ten minutes' more walking. I've lost a lot of weight. My wife can't stop smiling."

5 a Read your article again and answer the questions about Manuel or Alex.

  1 Who had the idea?
  2 How much time does he spend doing exercise at the moment?
  3 What's his morning routine now?
  4 How has it changed his life?

b Ask and answer the questions about each other's articles.

6 What do you think about the ideas in the articles?

I tend to ...

1 a Which sentences from the articles are about Manuel? Which are about Alex?

  1 Then I generally have breakfast and a shower.
  2 He normally cycles for 25 minutes to wash the clothes.
  3 After a while he was doing several hours' walking every morning.
  4 Every week I do ten minutes' more walking.
  5 I got really stressed and sometimes only did it once or twice a week.
  6 I do three hours a day at the moment.
  7 I tend to get up at around six-thirty now and get straight on the cycle washer.
  8 The 29-year-old now starts each day with a 45-minute cycle ride.

b Which highlighted words or expressions from 1–8:

  1 mean usually? (x3)
  2 say how often you do things? (x3)
  3 say how long or when you do things? (x2)

2 Write six sentences about your habits – four true, and two false. Use these topics and your own ideas.

  • in the morning   • when you get up   • in the evening
  • after your work/studies   • before you go to sleep   • meals, food and drink
  • sports and exercise   • household chores

3 a Listen to each other's sentences. Can you guess which are false?

b Find out more about each other's habits. Do you do the same or different things?

I start each day with two or three cups of coffee.

But you don't like coffee!

OK, it's false.

So what do you do in the morning?

Well, I ...

6.2

Extreme weather

1 **a** Read the weather fact file. Find the highlighted words in the pictures. What's the most surprising fact for you?

b Have you experienced these kinds of weather? Which ones occur in your country or region?

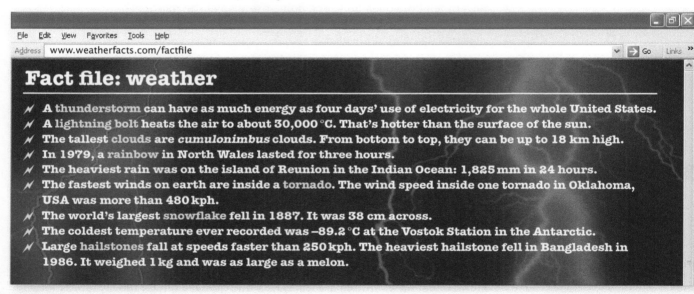

File   Edit   View   Favorites   Tools   Help

Address   www.weatherfacts.com/factfile   Go   Links »

Fact file: weather

- A thunderstorm can have as much energy as four days' use of electricity for the whole United States.
- A lightning bolt heats the air to about 30,000 °C. That's hotter than the surface of the sun.
- The tallest clouds are *cumulonimbus* clouds. From bottom to top, they can be up to 18 km high.
- In 1979, a rainbow in North Wales lasted for three hours.
- The heaviest rain was on the island of Reunion in the Indian Ocean: 1,825 mm in 24 hours.
- The fastest winds on earth are inside a tornado. The wind speed inside one tornado in Oklahoma, USA was more than 480 kph.
- The world's largest snowflake fell in 1887. It was 38 cm across.
- The coldest temperature ever recorded was −89.2 °C at the Vostok Station in the Antarctic.
- Large hailstones fall at speeds faster than 250 kph. The heaviest hailstone fell in Bangladesh in 1986. It weighed 1 kg and was as large as a melon.

2 **a** What problems do you think people can have when the weather's really hot, or really cold?

b ◆ 2.13 Listen to Jeevan and Vasily talking about the weather where they live.

   1   What kinds of weather do they talk about?
   2   Who talks about these things?

   • afternoons • driving • air conditioning
   • clothes • drinks • temperature • tourists

Jeevan from Kolkata

3 **a** Can you remember what Jeevan and Vasily say about the things in 2b? Talk together.

b ◆ 2.13 Listen again to check.

4 What do you do when the weather's really hot or cold? Do you like this kind of weather?

Vasily from Moscow

It isn't as cold as ...

GRAMMAR

Comparing things

1 a What are the comparatives and superlatives of the adjectives in the table?

One syllable	Two syllables ending in -y	Two or more syllables	Irregular
cold hot large	heavy	careful important	good bad far

colder, the coldest

b Use words from 1a to complete the sentences from the talks and the fact file.

Comparatives and superlatives	as ... as ...
You have to be _____ on the roads. That's _____ than the surface of the sun. The _____ hailstone fell in Bangladesh in 1986. The _____ thing is to drink a lot.	It weighed 1 kg and was as _____ as a melon. It isn't as _____ as Siberia.

c ◀ 2.14 Listen to check. ℗

2 Look at sentences 1–5. Which highlighted expression(s) means:

a big difference?   a small difference?   exactly the same?

1   It's usually –5 to –10 °C but it can get a lot colder.
2   People prefer to go to much hotter countries.
3   You should be a bit more careful in the hot sun.
4   Moscow is almost as cold as Siberia.
5   Helsinki is just as cold as Moscow.

3 Complete the paragraph about Pakistan with these adjectives in the correct form.

~~large~~   big   frightening   hot   cold (x2)   heavy

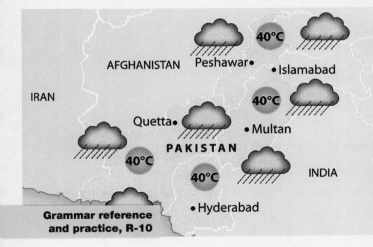

When I was little, I lived in Lahore in Pakistan. It's the second [1] *largest* city in Pakistan after Karachi. The weather in Lahore is extreme during the summer. The [2] _____ months are May, June and July, when temperatures can rise to 40–45 °C. The [3] _____ rainfall is in July and August during the monsoon. The [4] _____ months are December, January and February, but it doesn't often get [5] _____ than 9 °C. What I remember most clearly is the hail. Hailstones almost as [6] _____ as tennis balls would hit our house. They could break windows and damage cars. However, the [7] _____ moments were the dust storms, when the sky turned black in the middle of the day.

Grammar reference and practice, R-10

PRONUNCIATION

Words with -er and -est

4 a When a word ends in -er or -est, the stress stays on the same syllable. Say these words.

hot → hotter → the hottest   heavy → heavier → the heaviest

b Practise saying the comparatives and superlatives in 1a with the correct stress.

SPEAKING

5 a Think about these things in your country or another country you know. Make notes.

• climate and seasons   • extreme weather and storms
• oceans or seas   • rivers and lakes   • mountains

wettest – January and February
longest river – the Nile

In Dubai, the wettest months are January and February.

Actually, I think it's just as wet in December.

b Compare your ideas in groups. If you're from the same country, do you agree?

6.3　Target activity

Do a survey

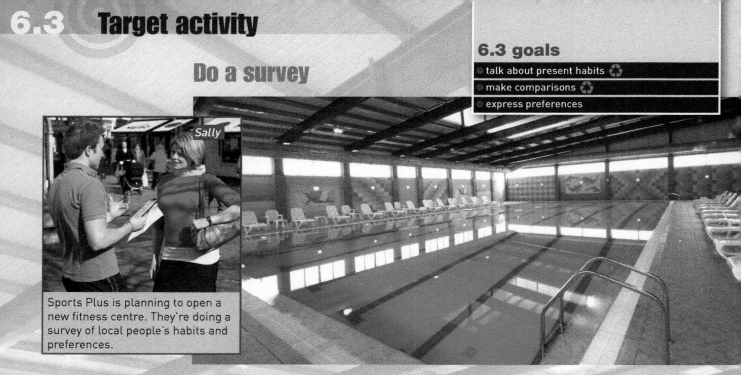

Sports Plus is planning to open a new fitness centre. They're doing a survey of local people's habits and preferences.

TASK LISTENING

1　Is there a fitness centre near where you live? What can you do there? Do you ever use it?

2　**2.15** Listen to the interview with Sally.

1　What does Sally think of the fitness centre she visits?
2　How often does she go there?
3　How long does she spend there?
4　What does she usually do?

TASK VOCABULARY

Expressing preferences

3　**a** Can you remember what Sally says? Complete the sentences with words from the box.

| a nicer pool　facilities　showers　women-only classes　changing rooms　pool |

1　The _____'s OK, but it could be bigger.
2　I'd prefer _____ as well.
3　The _____ could definitely be better.
4　I don't mind the _____.
5　I'd much rather have private _____.
6　I'd rather have _____ than a sauna.

b **2.15** Listen again to check.

4　Cover the sentences and look at the things in the box. Try to remember what Sally says.

TASK

5　**a** You decide to open a new business. In groups, choose one of the following or your own idea.

- a fitness centre　• a music shop　• a café or restaurant　• a market stall

b Before you open your business, you want to know about people's habits and preferences. Design a questionnaire with six questions. Think about these things.

- the kind of products / facilities / service　• location
- hours　• special features　• other ideas

*Do you ... ?　Where ... ?　When ... ?　Are you interested in ... ?　How often ... ?
How long ... ?　What do you ... ?　Do you prefer ... ?*

> How often do you go to a sports centre?
>
> Well, I go swimming once a week.

6　Use your questionnaire to interview people from other groups. Talk to three different people each.

7　**a** Go back to your group and compare your results. What kind of service would most people like?

b Tell the class about your decisions.

Keyword do

1 Put the highlighted collocations with do into three groups:

   a work and studies   b chores   c sports and exercise

```
1   Doing the vacuuming may be a better way to keep fit than swimming. Unit 6
2   These days we have to do our jobs and do exercise to stay healthy! Unit 6
3   In your home, who does the food shopping? Unit 3
4   I hated doing exams and tests and so on. Unit 2
5   I've done courses in music, local history and Spanish. Unit 2
6   I do a lot of work in the rainforest, in the Central Amazon. Unit 2
7   When I was at college, I did aerobics. Unit 1
```

2 **a** Make questions with the collocations in 1.

    Have you ever … ? How often do you … ? When was the last time you … ?

    Have you ever done yoga?

  b Ask and answer the questions together.

3 **a** Continue sentences 1–6 with a–f.

    do + a bit of/a lot of/some + activity
    1 I did a bit of singing when I was younger.   a I left my key in the door!
    2 I'm doing a lot of reading at the moment.   b The cleaning, the ironing, all the chores.
    3 When I'm stressed I do some yoga.   c The exercise really calms me down.
    do + something/anything/everything
    4 I did something really stupid last week.   d I'm half-way through a 500-page book.
    5 I didn't do anything last night.   e I was really into it.
    6 I have to do everything when my wife is away.   f I just came home and went to bed.

  b Write three more sentences about what you do.

    I did a bit of karate when I was at school.

  c In groups, read out your sentences. Ask questions to find out more.

Independent learning Reading the phonemic script

1 **a** Look at the dictionary entry for *routine*. How do you say it?

  b Work in pairs. How do you say these sounds?

    /b/ /f/ /m/ /θ/ /s/ /j/ /e/ /iː/ /ɪ/ /æ/ /ɔː/ /o/

  c Check with the chart on R-21.

> **routine** /ruːˈtiːn/ *noun* the things that you do every day at the same time: *a daily routine*

2 **a** Match the symbols 1–8 with the highlighted sounds in words a–h. Use the chart to help you.

  b 2.16 Listen to check. **P**

1	/iː/	a	her
2	/ʃ/	b	stay
3	/ʌ/	c	shopping
4	/e/	d	current
5	/eə/	e	best
6	/dʒ/	f	energy
7	/eɪ/	g	hair
8	/ɜː/	h	free

3 **a** In pairs, read the words 1–10.

    1 /dʒɪm/   6 /ˈkliː.nɪŋ/
    2 /ˈθʌn.də.stɔːm/   7 /ˈreɪn.bəʊ/
    3 /ˈsaɪklɪŋ/   8 /ˈvæk.juːmɪŋ/
    4 /tʃɔːʳz/   9 /tɔːˈneɪ.dəʊ/
    5 /klaʊdz/   10 /ˈwɔː.kɪŋ/

  b 2.17 Listen to check.

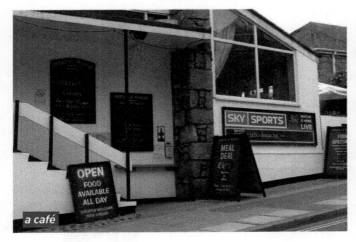

a café

a newsagent

a fitness centre

1 **2.18** Listen to three conversations. Match them with the pictures.

2 a You can be more polite by speaking less directly. Which sentences are less direct, a or b?

   1 a Would you mind answering some questions?
      b Can you answer some questions?
   2 a It could be better.
      b It's bad.

  b Look at the conversations. Find and <u>underline</u> the expressions that are less direct than these.

Requests
1 Can you answer a few questions?
2 Can you change this ten for me?
3 Can you tell me a bit more?

Refusing requests
4 No, I don't want to.
5 No, I don't need anything.

Opinions
6 The pool is dirty.
7 The staff aren't interested.
8 It's boring.
9 I'm not interested in football.

  c **2.19** Listen to check. ●

3 Make these expressions less direct using the words in (brackets). Then compare your answers.

1 My parents are old-fashioned. (a bit)
   My parents are a bit old-fashioned.
2 We're not hungry. (really)
3 Ronnie and Clara are unhappy. (don't seem)
4 I hate bananas. (really like)
5 George is stupid sometimes. (clever)
6 Can you wait for five minutes? (Would you mind)
7 Can you be quiet, please? (Do you think)
8 Can you help me with my bags? (I wonder if)

4 a **2.20** Listen to a phone conversation between André and Sue. Do you think it sounds polite?

  b Look at the script on R-19. In pairs, write a more polite version of the conversation. Practise it.

  c Listen to each other's conversations. Do you think they sound polite?

❶

BILL	Would you mind answering a few questions, please? It won't take long.
SHEILA	Er, yes, that's OK.
BILL	Thank you. Are you happy with the fitness centre generally?
SHEILA	Erm, well, it could be better.
BILL	Oh. I see. Do you think you could tell me a bit more?
SHEILA	Well, to be honest, the pool isn't always very clean. And the staff don't seem very interested.
BILL	Oh dear. Well, I'll definitely tell the manager.

❷

BEN	Hi. I wonder if you could change this ten for me. I need some coins for the ticket machine.
CLODAGH	Sorry, but I'd rather not. People are always asking me for change.
BEN	Oh.
CLODAGH	Perhaps you'd like to buy something?
BEN	Erm, no, not really.

❸

PHIL	Here's your drink. Sorry it took so long.
CATHERINE	So, what do you think of the game?
PHIL	Um, it's a bit boring.
CATHERINE	Boring?
PHIL	Well, you know I'm not really interested in football.
CATHERINE	So should we go? The second half starts in two minutes.
PHIL	No, you stay here. I'll do some shopping, then come back in an hour, OK?
CATHERINE	Well, OK. See you later.

Review

1 a Work in teams. Complete these weather words with vowels. Who can finish first?

rn thndrstrm lghtnng snwflk trnd
rnbw hlstns wnd clds tmprtr

b How did you feel about different kinds of weather when you were a child?

> When I was a child, I was afraid of lightning.

> Really? I thought it was exciting.

2 a Order the words in these questions.

1 life / in the past / Do you think / than / is easier now ?
2 it's better for children / Do you think / or / to play computer games / to read ?
3 cheerful / Who's / person you know / the most ?
4 better kinds of / than in the past / Do people have / entertainment ?
5 for you / the best place / What's / to relax ?
6 been to / the most exhausting event / What's / you've ever ?

b Ask and answer the questions. Give examples and reasons.

3 a Put the sentences of the conversation in order.

☐	ASSISTANT	Anything else?
☐	THIAGO	Next door? OK.
☐	ASSISTANT	<u>Eight postcards</u>. That comes to <u>six pounds forty</u>, please.
☐	THIAGO	No, that's all, thanks. How much is that?
☐	ASSISTANT	I'm afraid not, no. There's a cash machine just –
7	THIAGO	I'll take these <u>postcards</u>, please. And do you have any <u>maps</u>?
☐	THIAGO	No, it's OK, I've got some cash, I think.
☐	ASSISTANT	I'm sorry, we don't have any <u>maps</u> at the moment. You could try <u>next door</u>.
☐	ASSISTANT	Thank you. And that's <u>60 pence change</u>.
☐	THIAGO	Can I pay by card?

b Practise in pairs, changing the <u>underlined</u> expressions. Take turns to be Thiago and the shop assistant.

Extension

4 a 🔊 2.21 These two adjective endings sound the same, /əbl/. Read and listen.

comfort**able** avail**able** poss**ible** sens**ible**

b Complete these words to make endings with -ible or -able.

terr__ble fashion__ble imposs__ble
horr__ble memor__ble enjoy__ble

c 🔊 2.22 Spellcheck. Close your book. Listen to ten words and write them down.

d Look at the script on R-19 to check your spelling.

5 a Match these words with abbreviations from the weather fact file on p52.

1	millimetre	a	km
2	degrees (Celsius)	b	°C
3	kilometres per hour	c	cm
4	centimetre	d	mm
5	kilometre	e	kg
6	kilo (kilogram)	f	kph

b Can you remember what these figures are about? Talk together, then read to check.

1 38 cm   4 480 kph   6 −89.2 °C
2 18 km   5 1,825 mm   7 1 kg
3 30,000 °C

> I think 38 cm was the largest snowflake. It was 38 cm across.

c Talk together. Do you know, or can you guess:

1 how tall you are?
2 what the speed limit is for cars in your country?
3 how far it is from your home to the nearest airport?
4 what the temperature was on the hottest and coldest days you've had this year?
5 how much you weighed when you were born?

Self-assessment

Can you do these things in English? Circle a number on each line. 1 = I can't do this, 5 = I can do this well.

⊚ talk about present habits	1	2	3	4	5
⊚ talk about weather	1	2	3	4	5
⊚ make comparisons	1	2	3	4	5
⊚ express preferences	1	2	3	4	5
⊚ speak more politely by being less direct	1	2	3	4	5

• For Wordcards, reference and saving your work ›› e-Portfolio
• For more practice ›› Self-study Pack, Unit 6

7

City life

Sheikh Zayed Road in Dubai, 1991

Sheikh Zayed Road in Dubai, 2005

READING

1 Look at the pictures. What changes can you see?

2 Read the introduction to the article about urbanisation. Why do you think so many people around the world are going to live in cities?

---

www.viewpoint.com/urbanworld

Viewpoint – The urban world in 2050

In 1900, just 13 per cent of the world's people lived in cities. In 2008, the number passed 50 per cent for the first time in history. By 2050, the number will be about 70 per cent. The urban population in Asia and Africa will double, and there will be nearly 30 "megacities" – cities with more than 10 million people. So what will life be like for people in the cities of the future? Professor of human geography Ben Rhodes describes his vision of the urban world in 2050.

Professor Ben Rhodes

¹ Life in cities will be very different from how it is today. Energy, especially oil, will be very expensive, so many people will probably work at home, or have their workplaces close to where they live. There'll be less traffic on the roads, and it'll be easier for people to be close to their families. For these reasons cities won't have just one centre where everyone goes to work and shop. Instead, we'll probably see cities with many different centres.

² It will be difficult to provide enough water, gas and electricity for really big cities, so these will probably stop growing. Many people from the countryside will move to smaller cities of 500,000 people or less. Transport over long distances will be a lot more expensive than it is now, so people will have to use food and energy from the countryside around their cities.

They'll use local materials for building, and perhaps traditional styles of architecture too.

³ The thing I really worry about is that energy may become too expensive for many people. In the end we might have two groups of people: a rich group which can afford energy and lives in clean, green areas, and a bigger, poorer group which can't afford it and has to live in the more polluted parts of the city. This might lead to serious political problems.

⁴ As we all know, cities near the sea will probably experience some extra problems. As temperatures around the world go up, sea levels will rise and many places will have problems with flooding. Some cities will be OK, some may even find that the change in the climate is good for them, but others will need help. We really need to start planning for this now.

---

3 Read the rest of the article. In which paragraph 1–4 does Professor Rhodes talk about these topics?

a Cities and the countryside
b Cities near the sea
c Energy, money and politics
d Working and living in cities

4 Read the article again. What reasons does Professor Rhodes give for these predictions?

1 Cities will have many centres.
2 Big cities will stop growing.
3 Buildings will use local materials.
4 There might be political problems.
5 Some cities near the sea will need help.

5 In groups, ask and answer the questions.

1 How do you feel about the changes Professor Rhodes describes? Which are good and which are bad?
2 Do you disagree with anything Professor Rhodes says? Why?

VOCABULARY
The environment

6 Cover the article and use the words and expressions from the box to complete the sentences. Then check in the article.

> clean, green   climate   flooding   gas   oil
> polluted   sea levels   traffic   transport

1 Energy, especially _____, will be very expensive.
2 There'll be less _____ on the roads.
3 It will be difficult to provide enough water, _____ and electricity for really big cities.
4 _____ over long distances will be a lot more expensive.
5 We might have two groups of people: a rich group which lives in _____ areas …
6 … and a poorer group which has to live in the more _____ parts of the city.
7 As temperatures around the world go up, _____ will rise and many places will have problems with _____.
8 Some cities may find that the change in _____ is good for them, but others will need help.

SPEAKING

7 Ask and answer the questions.

1 Do you think the climate is changing around the world? What about where you live?
2 Which places in your country or city:

- have the worst traffic?   • sometimes have problems with flooding?
- have the most popular green areas?   • are the most polluted?
- might have problems if sea levels go up?

Making predictions

GRAMMAR
will, might, may

1 Read sentences 1–5. Then complete the grammar table with the highlighted words.

1 There'll be less traffic on the roads.
2 Cities won't have just one centre.
3 Big cities will probably stop growing.
4 Energy may become too expensive.
5 This might create two groups of people.

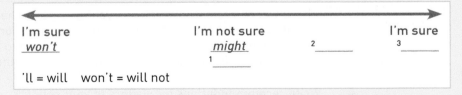

I'm sure	I'm not sure		I'm sure
won't	might	2 _____	3 _____
	1 _____		

'll = will   won't = will not

2 What do you think the world will be like in 2050? Make sentences with the words.

1 people / have / free time
2 families / have / children
3 children / study / home
4 people / use / cash / shops
5 food / expensive
6 people / do / exercise
7 English / important
8 people / happier

People will probably have less free time.

Grammar reference and practice, R-11

SPEAKING

3 a Think of three more predictions about life in 2050.

b Compare all your predictions from 2 and 3a in groups. Talk about your ideas.

If you're interested in art ...

READING

1 Look at the photos in the website for tourists. What do you know about Amsterdam?

2 Now read the entries. Which place would you most like to visit? Why?

GRAMMAR
Real conditionals

3 Complete the sentences from the website with words from the box.

'll (x2)   might   should

If + present,	will / might / should + infinitive
1 If you're interested in art,	you _____ love the Van Gogh Museum.
2 If you visit at the right time,	you _____ see more than seven million flowers.
3 If you want to eat here,	you _____ have to book in advance.
4 If you visit in the summer,	you _____ go to the house in the early evening.

4 Write recommendations for visitors to your country.

1 If you're interested in sightseeing, you'll love ...
2 If you want to do some shopping, you should go ...
3 If you enjoy trying new food, you might like ...
4 If you like the countryside, you'll ...
5 If you come in the winter, you should ...
6 If you like sports, you might ...
7 If you're interested in ...
8 If ...

Grammar reference and practice, R-11

SPEAKING

5 Listen to each other's recommendations. Which ones would you like to try? If you're from the same country, do you agree?

Getting directions

1 🔊 **2.23** Listen to Lizzy's conversation in the tourist office and answer the questions.

1 Where does she want to go? 2 How far is it?

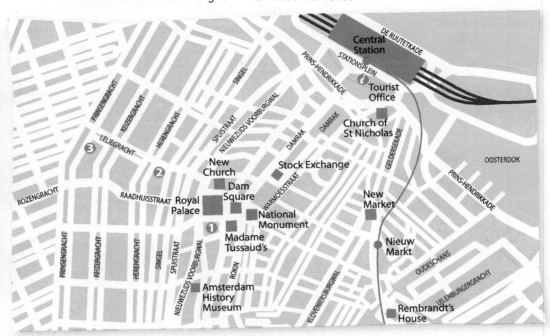

2 🔊 **2.23** Find the tourist office on the map and then listen again. Where's Anne Frank's house: 1, 2 or 3?

3 a Use the map to put the directions in order, 1–8.

Ask How can I get to Anne Frank's house?

Start We're next to the main train station.

- ☐ Go along Raadhuisstraat for about five hundred metres.
- ☑2 Go down the big street. It's called Damrak.
- ☑1 Go out of here and turn left.
- ☐ Turn right and go past the palace.
- ☐ When you get to the canal called Prinsengracht, turn right.
- ☐ If you continue along Damrak, you'll come to the Dam.
- ☑3 You'll go past a big building on your left, the Beurs.
- ☐ You'll see the National Monument on your left and the Royal Palace on your right.

Finish The house is by the canal.

b Check in the script on R-19. Then cover 3a, look at the map and give directions to Anne Frank's house.

4 a 🔊 **2.24** Listen and notice how the consonant and vowel sounds link in this sentence.

Go out‿of here‿and turn left.

b Mark the consonants and vowels that link in these directions.

1 Turn right and go past the palace. (x1)
2 You'll go past a big building on your left, the Beurs. (x2)
3 You'll see the National Monument on your left and the Royal Palace on your right. (x3)

c 🔊 **2.25** Listen to check. ℗ Practise saying the directions.

5 a Work alone. Choose two places on the map. Think about how to give directions from the tourist office.

b Listen to each other's directions and guess the places.

Get tourist information

7.3 goals
- make recommendations ♻
- give directions ♻
- get information in a tourist office

Sergei is in Amsterdam on business, but has some free time to see the city.

TASK LISTENING

1 a What can you remember about:

the Van Gogh Museum?   the Keukenhof Gardens?   Anne Frank's house?

b 🔊 2.26 Listen to Sergei's conversation in the tourist office. Which places does he decide to visit?

TASK VOCABULARY

Getting tourist information

2 a Can you remember what Sergei says? Tick (✓) the highlighted expressions he uses.

1   I'm looking for somewhere to stay.
2   Do you organise tours of the city?
3   Have you got a map?
4   Can you recommend some things to see?
5   Do you have any information about art galleries?
6   Do you sell tickets?

b 🔊 2.26 Listen again to check.

3 Can you think of more ways to continue the highlighted expressions in 2a? Use these and your own ideas.

- day trips • guidebooks • a leaflet • a restaurant
- the railway station • travel passes • a hotel

I'm looking for a good hotel.

TASK

4 a You're going to do a role play in a tourist office. Work in A/B pairs.

Student B, tell Student A the name of a neighbourhood, town or city you know well.
A, you're visiting this place. Think of five questions to ask.
B, you work in the tourist office. Decide where the tourist office is, then think of five things to recommend and how to get there.

b Have a conversation in a tourist office.

Hello, I'm looking for ...

A, start the conversation with one of your questions.
B, listen, make recommendations and give directions.

c Change roles and have another conversation.

Keyword *will*

will for predictions

1 a Put the lines of each conversation in the correct order, 1–3. 2.27 Then listen to check. Ⓟ

- ☐ It'll be Leona. I invited her for a coffee.
- ☐ Rob! Can you answer the door? I'm doing the washing up.
- ☐ Yeah, OK. Who is it?

- ☐ Ah, yes. How old is he?
- ☐ Don't forget, it's Deiter's birthday on Monday.
- ☐ He'll be twenty-five, I think.

b In which conversation is will ('ll):
  a about the future?   b about now?

c Write a list of five important people in your life. Then look at each other's lists and find out about the people. Use these questions and your own ideas.

1 Who are they? How do you know them?
2 Where do you think they are at the moment?
3 When will you see them again?
4 How do you think their lives will change in the next five years?

will for offers, promises, requests

2 a You can also use will to make:

offers

```
A   Can I put my case in the back?
B   I'll do that for you.  Unit 4
```

promises

```
OK, I'll give her the message and ask her to
contact you.  Unit 2
```

requests / orders

```
I'll take these postcards, please. And do you
have any maps?  Unit 5
```

Can you remember who said these sentences and where?

b 2.28 Listen to three short conversations. Which is:
  a a phone call?   b in a car?   c in a café?

c 2.28 Listen again. Think of a sentence with will to continue each conversation and then compare your ideas.

> Yes, I'll have some water, please.

Across cultures Tourism

1 a Read statements 1–6. Find a highlighted expression which means:

a a place where a lot of people go for holidays.
b the people who live in a place, not tourists.
c important places in a country's history.
d people's habits and ways of behaving.

1 Tourism helps people from different places to understand each other.
2 When you visit another country, you should try to speak the local language.
3 In a tourist resort, restaurants should sell food from tourists' countries *and* local food.
4 Tourism is bad for a country's areas of natural beauty and historical sites.
5 Visiting a place during a festival is a great way to learn about the customs and traditions there.
6 Tourism is good for the local people and local businesses.

b Tick (✓) the statements you agree with.

2 a 2.29 Listen to Natalie and Paula talking about statement 2. Do they generally agree or disagree with the statement?

b 2.29 What do they say are the good points about the statement? What are the problems? Listen again, then read the script on R-20 to check.

3 Tell each other what you think about statements 1–6. Explain your ideas.

7 EXPLOREWriting

1 a Choose a city, or a place you know well, to write about. Make a list of things you could write about.

buildings, parks, the weather ...

b Compare your ideas and add more things to your list.

2 a Read the web postings about home towns. Who writes about these things, Kelly, Madu or both of them?

1	people	3	flowers	5	the weather
2	homes	4	popular activities	6	the city's atmosphere

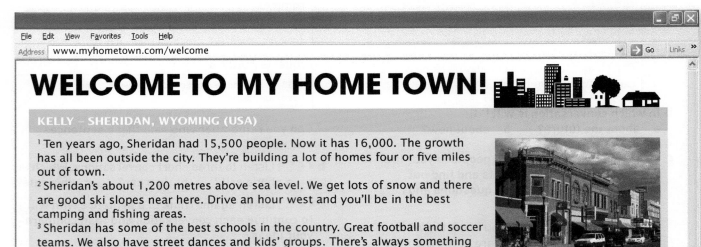

File   Edit   View   Favorites   Tools   Help

Address   www.myhometown.com/welcome

WELCOME TO MY HOME TOWN!

KELLY – SHERIDAN, WYOMING (USA)

¹ Ten years ago, Sheridan had 15,500 people. Now it has 16,000. The growth has all been outside the city. They're building a lot of homes four or five miles out of town.
² Sheridan's about 1,200 metres above sea level. We get lots of snow and there are good ski slopes near here. Drive an hour west and you'll be in the best camping and fishing areas.
³ Sheridan has some of the best schools in the country. Great football and soccer teams. We also have street dances and kids' groups. There's always something going on around here.

MADU – ABUJA (NIGERIA)

¹ In Nigeria, people often talk about the beauty of Abuja. It was a nice surprise when I stepped into this city for the first time. The city gate has many flowers planted around it. Nearby is the very modern National Stadium and the Games Village, which was used for the All African Games.
² Abuja is the federal capital city of Nigeria and a lot of the country's oil money has been spent on it. The streets and buildings look new, clean and beautiful.
³ There are modern houses and lots of trees and flowers. A nice wind blows in from the Sahara Desert. It's quiet and peaceful. After my first visit, I decided to make Abuja my home.

b Would you like to visit these places? Why? / Why not?

3 a Add words and expressions from the postings to these groups.

1 places and buildings *ski slopes, ...*
2 groups of people *football teams, ...*
3 events *street dances, ...*
4 the weather, nature *snow, ...*

b What words or expressions could you use to talk about your city? Add more things to each group.

4 a What adjectives do Kelly and Madu use? Try to complete the list, then check in the postings.

g*ood*   gr_____   ni_____   mo_____   ne_____
cl_____   be_____   qu_____   pe_____

b What adjectives could you use to talk about your city? Add them to the list.

5 a Plan a posting describing a place you know well.

1 Decide what things you want to talk about.
2 Organise the things into three or four paragraphs.
3 Think of words and expressions to use in each paragraph.

Look at the language in 3–4 and use your own ideas.

b Explain your ideas to each other.

6 Write your posting.

7 Read each other's postings. Ask questions to find out more information.

7 Look again ♻

Review

1 a Paul is talking about his life in the next five years. Put the words in order to make sentences.

   1   be happy have I I'll if job same the .
      I'll be happy if I have the same job.
   2   a annoyed be better can't car get I I'll if .
   3   be don't exams I I'll if my pass sad .
   4   be get I I'll if married surprised .
   5   be children have I I'll if shocked .

b Write sentences like 1–5 about your life in the next five years.

c Listen to each other's sentences. Ask questions to find out more.

VOCABULARY Giving directions

2 a 📢 2.30 Look at the map of a language school and listen to the receptionist's directions to a student. Where does the student go?

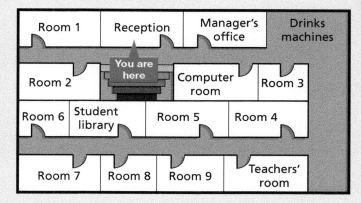

b Read the script on R-20 to check. Then look at the map and try to remember the directions.

c Take turns to ask for and give directions to other rooms from the reception. Listen and check the directions are correct.

CAN YOU REMEMBER? Unit 6 – Chores, habits

3 a Look at the sentence about chores. In groups, think of words or expressions which could replace each part of the sentence 1–4.

I <u>usually</u> <u>clean the windows</u> <u>once a</u> <u>month</u>.
    1   2   3   4
 tend to *do the ironing* *every* *day*

b Work alone. Think about how to describe a normal day in your life:

   • during the week.   • at the weekend.

c Tell each other about your days. Who spends the most time:

   at work? doing chores? studying? relaxing?

Extension

SPELLING AND SOUNDS *ui, uy*

4 a 📢 2.31 You can say *ui* and *uy* in three ways. Listen and repeat.

/ɪ/	/aɪ/	/uː/
build	buy	fruit

b Add these words to the correct group. Practise saying the words.

   guide suit guy juice guitar biscuit

c Circle the correct answer. Which letters do we use:

   1   in the middle of words? ui / uy
   2   at the end of words? ui / uy

d 📢 2.32 Spellcheck. Close your books. Listen to nine words and write them down. Then look at the script on R-20 to check your spelling.

NOTICE Noun + infinitive

5 a Complete the sentences from this unit with these nouns.

   place queue something
   somewhere things time

   1   The _____ to get in can be quite long.
   2   I'm looking for _____ to stay.
   3   One of the most popular _____ to see is Anne Frank's house.
   4   The best _____ to go is early evening.
   5   It's definitely a good _____ to visit.
   6   Would you like _____ to drink?

b Think about these questions. Then ask and answer in groups.

   1   Can you recommend a city to visit? When's the best time to go?
   2   In the city, can you recommend:
      a   somewhere to stay?
      b   some things to see? Are there long queues to get in?
      c   somewhere to have a meal?

Self-assessment

Can you do these things in English? Circle a number on each line. 1 = I can't do this, 5 = I can do this well.

◉ make guesses and predictions	1	2	3	4	5
◉ make recommendations	1	2	3	4	5
◉ give directions	1	2	3	4	5
◉ get information in a tourist office	1	2	3	4	5
◉ write a description of a place	1	2	3	4	5

• For Wordcards, reference and saving your work » e-Portfolio
• For more practice » Self-study Pack, Unit 7

Activities

Unit 1, p12, An unusual athlete 8b (Student A)

Michelle Sung Wie
– (be) Korean-American professional golfer
– (be) born in Honolulu, Hawaii in 1989
– (begin) playing golf at the age of four
– (win) two major golf tournaments in Hawaii at the age of 11
– (become) a professional player at 15
– (be) 185cm tall and very strong
– (train) hard every day
– (want) to play in the Masters one day
– (prepare) for a tournament at the moment

Read the information about Michelle. Think about these questions.

1   What does she do?
2   How did she get into golf?
3   What's she doing at the moment?

Unit 2, p24, Explore speaking 5a (Student A)

Role card 1
You work for CSP.
Answer the phone and:
o explain that the person is not there
o take the caller's contact details and a message.

Unit 2, p24, Explore speaking 5b (Student A)

Role card 3
You work for Findajob. You want to find out about an ex-employee of CSP, Andy Koch.
Your name: Mukami Lelei
Your phone number: 0481 301 991
Your email address: m.lelei@findajob.com.au
Call CSP and:
o say you want to talk to Mrs McLachlan. You want to find out about an ex-employee, Andy Koch.
o leave your contact details and a message.

Unit 4, p37, Telling a story 6a

   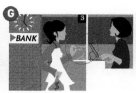 

Unit 4, p39, Independent learning 2b

1   Change the language on your computer to English.
2   Change the language on your mobile phone to English.
3   Listen to English radio programmes and podcasts.
4   Listen to English songs. Find the words on the Internet.
5   Make cards with English words on one side and a definition / picture on the other. Test yourself.
6   Make recordings of new English words and expressions. Listen to them on your way to work / school.
7   Meet your classmates half an hour before class begins. Chat in English.
8   Practise reading aloud a short text with the correct sounds and stress.
9   Read books in English. These can be special books for students, or children's books.
10 Visit Internet chatrooms for students of English.
11 Watch English-language films with subtitles in your own language.
12 Watch English-language TV programmes with a story – for example, soap operas.
13 Watch films with subtitles in English.
14 Write a diary in English. Write every day or every few days.
15 Write down new English words and expressions in a notebook. Read through them every few days.

Unit 5, p43, How would you like to pay? 6a (Student A)

CONVERSATION 1
You're a customer in a small shop.

Tick (✓) three things you'd like to buy.
postcards of Glasgow
stamps
a drink
a local newspaper
a sandwich
a phone card

You'd like to pay by card.
You have cash, but only a £50 note.

CONVERSATION 2
You're a receptionist in a museum.

You sell:
tickets £10 (adults) £6 (children) £4.50 (students, over-65s)
guided tours £2.50 extra
museum guidebooks £1.99 each
postcards £1.50 each
books about Glasgow's history £10 each

You don't have:
maps of Glasgow
stamps

You take cash or cards.
You don't have any bags.

Activities

Unit 1, p12, An unusual athlete 8b (Student B)

Vincent Mantsoe
- (be) a dancer, choreographer and teacher
- (be) born in Soweto, South Africa
- as a boy (dance) with youth clubs, practising street dances
- (copy) dance moves from videos
- (train) with the Johannesburg Moving into Dance company
- (create) own style of dance, called Afro-fusion
- now (have) his own international company of dancers
- the company (include) dancers from France, South Africa, the USA and Japan
- (prepare) a big new show at the moment

Unit 5, p45, Microcredit 6b (Student B)

http://www.microcreditsummit.org/stories/rukmani.htm

BORROWER SUCCESS STORIES
MICROCREDIT SUMMIT CAMPAIGN

"I had eleven children. Life wasn't easy," says Rukmani from Bidar in India. "There were days when we didn't have any food.

"When my children got married and left home, I got a loan of 200 rupees, and bought some pieces of metal from the shop where my husband worked. We used the metal to make useful things like knives. Then we sold them and made a profit.

"With a second loan, I started a small shop. Now my husband and I work together in the shop and make up to 100 rupees a day."

Unit 6, p50, Burning calories 4b

The cycle washer

Have you ever felt that there aren't enough hours in the day? These days we have to do our jobs, look after our homes, save energy to help the environment, and do exercise to stay healthy! Like many of us, Alex Gadsden never had enough time. He ran a business and a home and needed to lose weight. So he decided to do something about it. He invented the cycle washer.

The 29-year-old now starts each day with a 45-minute cycle ride. He not only feels healthier but he saves on his energy bills and does the washing too.

He said, "It gives the user a good workout. I've only used it for two weeks but I've already noticed a difference."

"I tend to get up at around six-thirty now and get straight on the cycle washer. I keep it in the garden, so it's nice to get out in the fresh air. Afterwards, I feel full of energy. Then I generally have breakfast and a shower and I really feel ready to start the day."

The green washing machine uses 25 litres of water a wash, and takes enough clothes to fill a carrier bag. He normally cycles for 25 minutes to wash the clothes, and then for another 20 minutes to dry them. And it doesn't use any electricity, of course.

Mr Gadsden, the boss of a cleaning company, believes his machine could become very popular. With an invention which cleans your clothes, keeps you fit and reduces your electricity bill, he may well be right.

5 a Read your article again and answer the questions about Alex.

1 Who had the idea?
2 How much time does he spend doing exercise at the moment?
3 What's his morning routine now?
4 How has it changed his life?

Unit 2, p24, Explore speaking 5a (Student B)

Role card 2
You are Jake Sanders and you work for Findajob.
Call CSP and:
- say you want to talk to Sara Moore. You want to find out about an ex-employee, Megan Simmons.
- leave your contact details and a message.
Your phone number: 0443 657 234
Your email address: j.sanders@findajob.com.au

Unit 5, p43, How would you like to pay? 6a (Student B)

CONVERSATION 1
You're an assistant in a small shop.

You sell:
postcards of Glasgow 80p each
books of 12 stamps £3.50 each
local newspaper £1.20 each
phone cards £5 or £10 each

You don't have:
drinks
sandwiches

You don't take cards, only cash.
You don't want any big notes.

CONVERSATION 2
You're a visitor to a museum.

Choose the kind of ticket you want.
an adult ticket, a child ticket (under 18),
a student ticket, a senior citizen ticket (over 65)

Tick (✓) three more things you'd like to buy.
a museum guidebook
a guided tour of the museum
a map of Glasgow
a book about Glasgow's history
postcards
stamps

You'd like to pay by card.
You'd like a bag.

Unit 2, p24, Explore speaking 5b (Student B)

Role card 4
You work for CSP.
Answer the phone and:
- explain that the person is not there
- take the caller's contact details and a message.

Unit 3, p27, Food and you 5

basil cheese chicken cream curry fruit herbs lasagne

mushrooms salad sauces spices strawberries vegetables

Unit 3, p28, Eating out 4

bread cake cucumber ice cream oil olives pasta a pear

potatoes prawns rice salmon soup steak tomatoes

Unit 3, p32, Explore writing 2

Verbs for preparing

chop cut pour serve shake stir

Verbs for cooking

bake boil fry grill roast toast

Grammar reference and practice

1 PRESENT SIMPLE, PAST SIMPLE, PRESENT PROGRESSIVE

MEANING

You can vhappen all the time.
I live in Frankfurt in Germany.
I play tennis with my sister every weekend.

You can use the past simple to talk about things that are in the past and finished.
When I was fifteen, I decided to be a doctor.
I studied for seven years.

You can use the present progressive to talk about things happening now, or around now.
Sorry, I can't go out now. I'm waiting for a phone call.
I'm reading a really interesting book about the history of Turkey.

FORM

	present simple	past simple	present progressive
❓	Where do you live?	What did you study?	What are you waiting for?
➕	I live in Frankfurt.	I studied medicine.	I'm waiting for a phone call.
➖	I don't live in Berlin.	I didn't study languages.	I'm not waiting for you.
❓	Do you play tennis?	Did you have a good weekend?	Are you listening to me?
✔	Yes, I do.	Yes, I did.	Yes, I am.
✘	No, I don't.	No, I didn't.	No, I'm not.

Remember...
(1) In the present simple, verbs with *he / she / it* have s or es.
Where does he live? He lives in Frankfurt. He doesn't live in Berlin.
Does he play tennis? Yes, he does. No, he doesn't.

(2) In the past simple, some verbs are regular and others are irregular.
Regular: *play > played   decide > decided   study > studied*
Irregular: *be > was / were   have > had   go > went*

(3) In the present progressive, you can make negatives in two ways.
You aren't listening to me. You're not listening to me.
No, you aren't. No, you're not.

But there's only one kind of negative with *I*.
I'm not talking to you.
No, I'm not.

PRONUNCIATION

Question words and main verbs usually have stress.
Where do you live?   I live in Frankfurt.

But in negative sentences and short answers, do / did / be or not also have stress.
I didn't study languages.   You aren't listening to me.
Yes, he does.   No, I'm not.

PRACTICE

1 **Complete the sentences with the correct form of the verb.**

  1 Why don't you call Alain now? He usually __*finishes*__ (finish) work early on Fridays.
  2 It (rain) _____ all day yesterday so we _____ (decide) to stay at home.
  3 Ahmed _____ (not work) today. He's ill.
  4 I _____ (not drive), so I usually walk to places when I can, or get buses.
  5 I _____ (see) Helena in town yesterday. And guess what? She _____ (get) married last month.
  6 Can we make something vegetarian? Pam _____ (not eat) meat.
  7 Sorry, Petra _____ (talk) to a client at the moment. Can you phone back later?
  8 When I _____ (be) a child, we _____ (not have) a lot of money, so we _____ (not go) to restaurants.

2 **a Complete the questions with** do, does, did **or** are.

  1 How often __*do*__ you cook for more than two people?
  2 When _____ you have your first English lesson?
  3 What time _____ you usually go to bed?
  4 What _____ you doing at work these days?
  5 Where _____ you get your watch?
  6 How _____ you meet your oldest friend?
  7 How often _____ it snow in your home town?
  8 How many books _____ you reading at the moment?

b Ask and answer the questions.

2 PRESENT PERFECT 1 – FOR EXPERIENCE

MEANING

You can use the present perfect to talk about experiences up to now, from past to present.
I've seen all Almodóvar's films.
Oh really? I haven't seen any of them.

Don't use the present perfect with finished times in the past.
I've been to Tokyo four years ago. I went to Tokyo four years ago.
I've seen Jane last week. I saw Jane last week.

You can use ever in questions and negatives. Ever means 'in my / your whole life'.
Have you ever been to Japan?
I haven't ever been to Germany.

FORM

have / has + past participle.

I, you, we, they	he, she, it
➕ I've seen all Almodóvar's films.	➕ She's visited more than twenty countries.
➖ We haven't met Jane's husband. We've never met Jane's husband.	➖ He hasn't done a computer course. He's never used a computer.
❓ Have they been to Japan? Yes, they have. No, they haven't.	❓ Has he taken his driving test? Yes, he has. No, he hasn't.

Contractions:
➕ I've = I have   you've = you have   we've = we have
they've = they have
he's = he has   she's = she has   it's = it has

➖ haven't = have not
hasn't = has not

Some past participles are regular and end in *-ed*. They're the same as the past simple.
like > liked   smoke > smoked   visit > visited

Some past participles are irregular but the same as the past simple.
buy > bought   have > had   meet > met

Some past participles are irregular and different from the past simple. They often end with *n*.
eat > ate > eaten   do > did > done   see > saw > seen

See *Irregular verbs* on R-22.

PRONUNCIATION

You usually stress the past participle.

You don't usually stress have / has in positive sentences and questions.

I've seen all Almodóvar's films.   Has he met Jane?

But you usually stress have / has in negative sentences and short answers.

We haven't met Jane's husband.   Yes, they have.   No, she hasn't.

You often say *been* as /bɪn/.

PRACTICE

1 **a Complete these sentences with the verbs in (brackets) in the present perfect or past simple.**

1 A Have you ever _been_ to India?
  B Yes, I _went_ there in 2006. (go)
2 A Have you _____ any Brazilian films?
  B Yes, I've _____ *City of God.* (see)
3 A Have you ever _____ anything creative?
  B Well, I _____ some short stories a few years ago. (write)
4 A Have you _____ any computer courses?
  B Yes, I _____ one on web design when I was a student. (do)
5 A What languages have you _____ ?
  B Well, I _____ English and German at school. (study)
6 A Have you ever _____ a politician?
  B Yes, I _____ my local politician last year. (meet)

b Ask the questions and give your own answers.

PRESENT PERFECT 2 – WITH *FOR* AND *SINCE*

MEANING

You can also use the present perfect to talk about situations which began in the past and continue in the present.
I've lived here for ten years.
I haven't eaten since breakfast.

FORM AND PRONUNCIATION

See *present perfect 1 – for experience.*

PRACTICE

1 **a Add for or since to these sentences.**

　　　　　　　　　　　　　　　　　　　　　since
1 My parents have lived in the same house ⁄ they got married.
2 My mum's had the same hairstyle about fifteen years.
3 I've had the same computer five years.
4 There hasn't been any snow in my country 2008.
5 I've known my best friend school.
6 My brother's worked at the same company he left university.

b Make the sentences true for you. Then compare with a partner.

3 NOUNS WITH PREPOSITIONAL PHRASES

MEANING

You can use prepositional phrases to give extra information about nouns.
Let's go to the restaurant. Which restaurant? *The restaurant in the town centre.*
I'd like the salad. Which salad? *The salad with blue cheese.*
Can you give me my book? Which book? *The book on the table.*

FORM

Prepositional phrases can go *after a noun*.
      noun   prepositional phrase
Let's go to the restaurant in the town centre.

Adjectives usually go *before a noun*.
    adjective noun
Let's go to the Italian restaurant.

You can use adjectives and prepositional phrases together.
    adjective noun   prepositional phrase
Let's go to the Italian restaurant in the town centre

prepositional phrase
next to the cinema.

PRONUNCIATION

You usually stress the nouns, not the prepositions.

The restaurant in the town centre.

The salad with blue cheese.

The book on the table.

You usually say the prepositions of, for and to as /əv/, /fə/ and /tə/ in sentences.

PRACTICE

1 Complete the sentences with from, in, on or with.

1 *Churrasco* is grilled meat __*with*__ salt and garlic.
2 This is Rajeev, my friend _____ work.
3 Let's go to the coffee shop _____ the corner.
4 I usually have my tea _____ milk.
5 The food _____ that supermarket is cheap.
6 The girl _____ blonde hair is my sister.
7 Do you know the man _____ the grey suit?
8 He has a house _____ a small garden.
9 The hotel _____ the hill has a great view.
10 The market _____ the town centre is good for fresh fruit.

2 a Put the words in order to make sentences.

1 in red wine sauce / sounds nice / Steak. *Steak in red wine sauce sounds nice.*
2 with potatoes / is / Grilled salmon / my favourite dish .
3 today / the cheese plate / Do you have / with fruit bread ?
4 tomato / is / The soup of the day / with basil .
5 fresh fruit salad / I'd like the / for dessert, please / with cream .
6 with milk and sugar / please / two coffees / Can we have ?

b What do you think of the dishes and drinks in 2a? Would you order them in a restaurant?

4 PAST PROGRESSIVE

MEANING

You can use the past progressive to talk about an action that was in progress at a time in the past.

I started making the dinner at 5.30 pm.
At 6.00 pm I was making the dinner. (point in time = 6.00 pm)
The dinner was ready at 7.00 pm

I left work at 4.00 pm.
When you phoned me, I was driving home. (point in time = when you phoned me)
I got home at 4.20 pm.

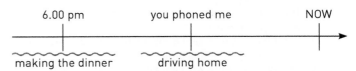

Compare the past simple and the past progressive:
I made the dinner yesterday. (talking about a finished action)
At 6 pm yesterday, I was making the dinner. (saying an action was in progress at a time in the past)

When she phoned me, I drove home. (She phoned me, and then I drove home.)
When she phoned me, I was driving home. (She phoned me in the middle of my journey home.)

FORM

was / were + -ing

❷ What were you doing at 6 pm yesterday?	❷ Were you driving home when I called?
➕ I was making the dinner.	➕ Yes, I was.
➖ I wasn't watching TV.	➖ No, I wasn't.

Remember:
I / he / she / it was
you / we / they were

PRONUNCIATION

In positive sentences and questions, you don't usually stress was and were. We say /wəz/ and /wə/.
In negative sentences and short answers, you usually stress was and were. We say /wɒz/ and /wɜː/.

Who was making the dinner?   I was making the dinner.

You weren't making the dinner.

Yes, I was.

PRACTICE

1 Complete the sentences with the verbs in brackets in the past progressive.

1 We first met Jim and Esin when we __*were travelling*__ in Turkey. (travel)
2 What _____ you _____ when I called you? There was no answer. (do)
3 It _____ when I left my flat this morning. Now it's hot and sunny. (rain)
4 My brother _____ the computer so I used it to check my email. (not use)
5 "Where's Ben?" "He _____ in the garden about an hour ago." (play)
6 I saw an accident when I _____ to work this morning. (drive)

7 _____ Pedro _____ his homework when you saw him? (do)

8 I went home at about two o'clock yesterday. I _____ well. (not feel)

2 Circle the best verb form in each sentence.

1 I went / was going to bed at two in the morning but ...

2 ... I couldn't sleep. My neighbours had / were having a party.

3 Sorry, can you say that again? I didn't listen / wasn't listening.

4 When I was younger, my family lived / was living in Berlin for three years.

5 The family had / were having lunch when the police arrived / were arriving.

6 The last time I saw / was seeing Joanna, she lived / was living in Paris.

7 I first met / was meeting my husband when I stood / was standing at a bus stop.

8 We worked / were working abroad when we had / were having our first child.

5 HAVE TO, CAN

MEANING

Use have to to say that something is necessary (now, in the future or in general).
Sorry, but I have to go now. My taxi's waiting for me. (now)
I have to get up at five o'clock tomorrow morning. My train leaves at ten past six. (in the future)
On a normal working day I have to be at the office before nine-thirty. (in general)

Use don't / doesn't have to to say something is not necessary.
Please start eating. You don't have to wait for me.

Use can to say that something is possible (now, in the future or in general).
You can use my phone if you want. (now)
We can meet again next weekend if you have time. (in the future)
You can pay your phone bill at the post office or on the Internet. (in general)

Use can't to say something is not possible.
I'd like to buy a flat but I can't get a loan from the bank.

FORM

I, you, we, they	he, she, it
➕ I have to go now.	Alain has to get up early tomorrow.
➖ I don't have to go until ten.	Rebecca doesn't have to get up until nine.
❓ Do you have to go so soon?	Does Rebecca have to work tomorrow?
✔ Yes, I do.	Yes, she does.
✘ No, I don't.	No, she doesn't.

I, you, he, she, it, we, they
➕ You can get married when you're 18.
➖ You can't get married when you're 16.
❓ Can you get married when you're 16?
✔ Yes, you can.
✘ No, you can't.

PRONUNCIATION

You usually stress have / has but not to. Have to and has to are often pronounced /ˈhæftə/ and /ˈhæstə/.
I have to go.

You don't usually stress can in positive sentences and questions. You say /kən/.
You can use my phone.   Can you smoke when you're sixteen?

You usually stress can in negative sentences and short answers. You say /kæn/ and /kɑːnt/.
Yes, you can. /kæn/

You can't drive when you're fourteen.   No, you can't. /kɑːnt/

PRACTICE

1 Complete the sentences with the correct form of can or have to, positive or negative.

1 Is there a cash machine near here? I _____ get some money.

2 "Can I make myself a cup of coffee?" "Of course you can. You _____ ask."

3 Where I live, you _____ buy anything after five p.m. All the shops are closed.

4 Carlo's not coming to work this morning. He _____ go to the doctor's.

5 OK, I can hear you! You _____ shout!

6 People think Poland's a cold country, but summers in Poland _____ be really hot.

7 Our company likes its employees to dress smartly. You _____ wear jeans, and men _____ wear a tie.

8 Sorry, I _____ meet you for lunch tomorrow. I _____ go to work.

2 a Order the words to make questions.

1 do get up have to on a typical day What time you ?
What time do you have to get up on a typical day?

2 Can manage online you your bank account ?

3 at weekends do have to How often work or study you ?

4 children in your country do go have to How many years to school ?

5 join people in your country Can the army when they're 16 ?

6 Do English ever have to for your work or studies use you ?

7 do do have to tomorrow What things you ?

8 go students in your country to university without paying Can ?

b Discuss the questions.

6 COMPARING THINGS

MEANING

Monday	Tuesday	Wednesday	Thursday
28°C	24°C	24°C	19°C

Comparatives

Monday was sunnier than Tuesday.
Thursday's weather was much cooler than Monday's.

Superlatives

Monday's weather was the hottest and sunniest.
Thursday's was the coldest and wettest.

as ... as

Tuesday was as warm as Wednesday.
Tuesday wasn't as warm as Monday.

FORM

Spelling rules	Adjective	Comparative	Superlative
most one-syllable adjectives	fast	faster	the fastest
one-syllable adjectives ending in one short vowel + a consonant	big	bigger	the biggest
most two-syllable adjectives	careful	more careful	the most careful
two-syllable adjectives ending in –y	happy	happier	the happiest
adjectives with three syllables or more	comfortable	more comfortable	the most comfortable

Some common irregular comparatives and superlatives are:
good – better – best
bad – worse – worst
far – further – furthest

PRONUNCIATION

You usually stress more and adjectives. You don't stress than and -er. You say /ðən/ and /ə/.

This camera's more expensive than my old one.

It's harder working at home than in an office.

You usually stress most and adjectives. You don't stress the and -est. You say /ðə/ and /ɪst/.

This is the most comfortable room in my flat.

I'm the tallest in my family.

But when *the* is in front of a word starting with a vowel, we pronounce it with an /iː/.

  iː   iː
the earliest   the oldest

You don't usually stress *as*. You say /əz/.

I don't think you're as tall as me.

PRACTICE

1 **Complete the sentences with the correct form of the adjectives.**

1 It's much _____ (wet) in the north of the country than in the south.
2 He's _____ (relaxed) person I know.
3 Amie is much _____ (happy) now than she was.
4 Jaynie is as _____ (good) at her job as Matt is.
5 He's much _____ (energetic) than I am.
6 That's the _____ (bad) meal I've ever had here.
7 This report isn't as _____ (interesting) as the last one.
8 Is this the _____ (good) hotel you could find?

2 **Order the words to make sentences.**

1 the / Running the marathon / is / difficult thing / I've ever done / most .
2 cheerful / when it's sunny / I'm usually / more .
3 getting a taxi / Getting a bus / is / easy / as / as .
4 frozen vegetables / good / I think / as / fresh ones / are / as .
5 intelligent / person I know / My brother / most / is / the .
6 worst / way to travel / Organised holidays / the / are .
7 to get fit / than / Doing exercise / a healthier way / is / dieting .
8 as / last summer / isn't / This summer / nice / as .

7 WILL, MIGHT, MAY

MEANING

You can use will to say you are sure about something in the future.
In 2050, 70% of people around the world will live in cities. (future)

But you can also use will to talk about now, or about things in general.
A Shall I phone Irina?
B No, call her later. She'll be at work now. (now)

I work with a really good team. If you have a problem, they'll always try to help. (in general)

You can use will with other words to show that you are more or less sure.
+++ *Brazil will definitely win the next World Cup.*
 ++ *Brazil will win.*
 + *Brazil will probably win.*
 ? *Maybe / Perhaps Brazil will win.*

You can use both might and may to say you're not sure about something.
A Shall we have a barbecue tomorrow?
B I'm not sure. It might / may rain. (future)

A Where's Irina?
B I don't know. She might / may be in a meeting. (now)

A Where's Lagos?
B I don't know. I think it might / may be in Nigeria. (in general)

May is a little more formal than might. May is more common in formal kinds of writing, but might is more common in everyday speech.

There is an important difference between might / may and can.
The supermarket might / may be crowded on Saturday. (I'm not sure if it will be crowded on Saturday.)
The supermarket can be crowded on Saturday. (I'm sure it is sometimes crowded on Saturday.)

FORM

will / might / may + infinitive without to

➕	➖	❓	✔/✘
It'll / It will rain.	It won't / will not rain.	Will it rain?	Yes, it will. / No, it won't.
It might rain.	It might not rain.	-	It might. / It might not.
It may rain.	It may not rain.	-	It may. / It may not.

PRONUNCIATION

You usually contract will like this: 'll /əl/ and won't /wəʊn(t)/.

You don't usually stress will / might / may.

Will Amy pass her exam next week?   *I think she'll try her best.*

They might cancel the party.

But you stress won't, not and short answers.

She won't pass.   *She might not pass.*   *She might.*

PRACTICE

Complete the sentences with will or might in the positive or negative.

1 A What are you doing tonight?
  B Nothing. I'm really tired so I __'ll__ just stay in.
2 A Where are you going?
  B Sorry, I just have to go to the bank. I _____ be long.
3 A Are Penny and Alex here yet?
  B No, they said they _____ be late. It depends on the traffic.
4 A Will you finish painting the kitchen today?
  B No, I'm tired. I _____ probably do it in the morning.
5 A Why isn't Jacob at work today?
  B I don't know. He hasn't called. He _____ be ill.
6 A Do you know where Ahmed is?
  B Yes, he _____ be in the café next door. He always has lunch there.
7 A Shall I give Lucy a call?
  B OK, but call her on her mobile. She _____ be at home until six.
8 A Can we meet again tomorrow?
  B I'm not sure. I'm pretty busy tomorrow so I _____ be able to see you.

REAL CONDITIONALS

MEANING

You can use real conditionals to do a lot of different things. For example:

If you want to visit this country, you have to get a visa.
(giving information)
If you're interested in ballet, you must see Carlos Acosta.
(recommending something)
If you're not feeling well, you can go home. (giving permission)
If you've worked here for five years, you should ask for a pay rise.
(giving advice / your opinion)
If I see Jeff tomorrow, I'll give him your phone number.
(making a promise)

In all these sentences, the speaker feels that the situation in the *if* part of the sentence (*If you want to visit this country...*, etc.) is real or possible.

FORM

Conditional sentences have two parts:

if-clause   main clause
***If** it rains tomorrow, **we**'ll stay at home.*

You can reverse the two parts. In this case you don't usually write a comma (,).

main clause   *if*-clause
***We**'ll stay at home **if** it rains tomorrow.*

PRONUNCIATION

The pronunciation of real conditionals is the same as in other sentences. For example, we usually stress verbs and nouns but not modal verbs or prepositions.

If it rains tomorrow, we'll stay at home.

PRACTICE

Circle the correct form of the verb.

1 Can you give me your mobile number? I call / 'll call you if I need / 'll need some help.
2 Don't worry if I 'm / 'll be late home tonight. I've got loads of work at the office.
3 You've worked really hard. I 'll be / 'm very surprised if you don't / won't pass the exam.
4 If you come / 'll come to Sao Paulo again, you come / must come and see us.
5 If you 're / 'll be interested in antiques, you love / 'll love this museum.
6 If there 's / 'll be a lot of traffic tomorrow , we leave / 'll leave home early.
7 If you go / 'll go to the shops later, do / will you get me a paper?
8 You leave / should leave now if you don't / won't want to be late.

1.1

Hi, my name's Kate Mori and I'm from Ottawa in Canada. I live with my husband, Masao, and, er, we have a cat. I'm a teacher. I work in a kindergarten. I speak English and French, and right now I'm studying Japanese, and slowly making progress! Er, I also study art history at night school once a week. Erm, I'm really interested in art, especially certain Canadian artists like Frank Johnston, so when I have the time, I like visiting the art galleries we have round here. Erm, Masao's interested in art too so we usually go together. What else? Well, sometimes I play tennis with my brother. He lives near me. And in the winter I go skating on the canal, which is a typical Ottawa thing to do!

1.2

INTERVIEWER So Kate, why are you learning Japanese?

KATE Well, last year I got married to Masao. He's from Japan.

I Congratulations.

K Thanks. So now I'm learning because I really want to talk with my husband's family, his parents and so on. They don't speak English …

I And you don't speak Japanese?

K Well, I can say 'hello' and 'goodbye', but I'd like to have a real conversation with them.

I Hm, so, does Masao teach you?

K No. He tried to give me some lessons but I just can't study at home. I can't concentrate.

I OK, so what do you do?

K Well, I didn't want to stop studying, so I started going to classes.

1.3

INTERVIEWER So Kemal, you're at university?

KEMAL Er, yes, I'm studying chemistry, but I also have Spanish lessons twice a week.

I Spanish?

K Yeah.

I And why is that?

K Because I like it.

I OK.

K You know, I've always liked learning languages. I sometimes need English for my studies but Spanish is my hobby, I guess. I like reading in Spanish.

I You mean books?

K Not books, no, but er, you know, things on the Internet, sometimes magazines. And I love Spanish cinema. One day I want to watch Spanish films without the subtitles.

I Have you ever been to Spain?

K Actually, no.

I Ah.

K I'd really like to go to Spain, of course, but maybe after I finish my studies here.

1.4

INTERVIEWER Erm, Natalie, did you have a lot of experience of music when you were little?

NATALIE I think I was very lucky, in that I came from Trinidad and Tobago, so when I was younger there was a lot of music around me all the time. Lots of different types of music. We did have music from the rest of the world but our local music is very special.

I Was that in your home, or just generally in the streets and … ?

N It's everywhere. You cannot get away from music in Trinidad. We have … we've created our own instrument called the steel drum. And you put … you take an oil drum and you hammer it and you get notes out of it. And they make huge orchestras … and I learned how to play the steel drum when I was a little girl.

I Do you have one?

N I have one in Trinidad, but they're very difficult to travel with.

I How, how big is it?

N Erm, I would say it's about – what's this? – half a metre wide, maybe, and probably a metre high.

I Right.

N And you play it with sticks, so I couldn't really travel with it. But Trinidad definitely has a lot of variety. We have a local music called calypso, which is similar to music from Latin America, er, sort of a merengue beat. And we have a lot of reggae, which probably you would have heard of, from Jamaica.

I What's your personal favourite?

N Erm, well I play classical piano. I was brought up to play classical piano, but nowadays I play more Cuban music on piano. Son, salsa, things like that, rumba.

I And do you still play the steel drum?

N I have forgotten some. I would love to

I So Sun-Hi, you're learning English.

SUN-HI Yes, I have a job with a large international company in Seoul, so I need English for my work.

I Hm, do you travel a lot?

S No, I don't need English for travel so much but, er, we have a lot of English-speaking visitors from other countries, especially Australia.

I Ah, I see.

S So I always talk to them in English. Of course we have a lot of visitors from other places too.

I Sure.

S Europe, other countries in Asia, but we usually speak in English.

I What about writing?

S Well, yes, my speaking's OK but I need to practise my writing. I read and write a lot of emails in English but it takes me a long time.

be able to play it again because I think it's very original and it has a lovely sound, but unfortunately I don't have it with me.

1.5

JOHN So, have you got any plans for the weekend?

CAMERON No, not really. You?

J Well, I was thinking about going to the festival, you know?

C WOMADelaide?

J Yeah, it starts on Friday. Do you want to go?

C Sure, if we can get tickets for a day or a night. I couldn't do the whole weekend.

J Me neither, it's too expensive. So when's best for you?

C Sunday probably. It doesn't really matter – it depends what's on.

J Yeah, and if there are any tickets left. Why don't we have a look online?

C OK, hang on a minute. Right. Sunday. Ah, Cesaria Evora's playing. She's amazing.

J Yeah, I'd love to see her. Or Mista Savona looks interesting.

C Hm, I'm not really into reggae.

J OK, well … er, erm … What do you think about this? The Terem Quartet?

C The folk? Yeah, that sounds good.

J Well, there's plenty of good stuff on Sunday. Do you want me to see if there are any tickets?

C Good idea. And do you want to ask anyone else? Maybe Jen?

J Yes, and Sally would probably like to come too. Maybe we could get a group together.

C Yeah, it would be a good laugh.

1.6

1 hockey, running, skiing, swimming, tennis, yoga
2 volleyball
3 aerobics, karate

1.7

INTERVIEWER So, how did you get into biking?

LI Well, it started when I was a kid. Er, my dad had a motorbike and I thought it looked like fun. Then I really got into motorbikes when I was a teenager. My first boyfriend also had a really nice bike, so we went riding in the countryside a lot and, yeah, it was great, er, but really I wanted to ride the bike, not sit on the back!

I OK, and what about now?

L Well, last year I wrote a book for children. Er, it was about a mother who rode a motorbike, a Harley-Davidson in fact, so I just had this motorbike idea in my head. Then I decided that I really wanted to learn something new. It didn't really matter what but I wanted to learn a new skill, you know, and the great thing about it is, it doesn't take very long to learn. So I saved up some money and I started having lessons.

I And how did that go?

L Well, it was a fascinating experience. It was very difficult at first, er, much harder than I expected, but I enjoyed it too. At times it was quite frightening – terrifying in fact! Er, I passed my test a few months ago and I'm much more relaxed now, but I still need to get a lot more experience.

I So, what is it that you like about being on a bike? Do you like going fast?

L No. I'm not interested in going fast. I love it because I feel free. I can go wherever I want to go, any time. So, no, for me, speed isn't important.

I Do you use your bike for getting around, getting to work … ?

L No, it's too dangerous. I've been into the town centre on my bike one or two times and there are so many cars, people, it's terrible. I really like riding in the countryside on big, empty roads where there are no cars. And as you ride along you can smell things – not, you know, cars, but the trees, flowers, the rain. That's what I really like about it.

■ 1.8

Write the name of a sport you're interested in, but don't play.
Write the name of a sport you did when you were younger, but don't do now.
Write the name of a sport you really don't like.
Write the name of a sport you like to watch on TV.
Write the name of a group or singer you'd like to see in concert.
Write the name of a group or singer you loved when you were younger.
Write the name of a group or singer you listen to a lot at the moment.
Write the name of a group or singer you really don't like.

■ 1.9

sport born motorbike doctor work

■ 1.10

1 normal	6 world
2 work	7 motorway
3 important	8 word
4 information	9 doctor
5 forty	10 orchestra

■ 1.11

1

INTERVIEWER Luis, you're twenty-nine …

LUIS Right.

I … and you're a student?

L Well, I work as an archaeologist but, yeah, I'm also a student, I guess.

I Right. What kind of archaeology do you do?

L I do a lot of work in the rainforest, in the Central Amazon.

I But right now you're doing a degree, aren't you?

L Yes, I'm doing a doctorate in archaeology. Actually, I'm writing a thesis on my work in the Amazon.

I And when do you finish?

L I've got just one more year to go – I hope!

I And will you stop then?

L Stop studying?

I Yes.

L Well, I think an archaeologist is always studying, so, no, I'll never stop. It's a way of life for me.

2

I Pierre, you didn't like school much. Why was that?

PIERRE Well, I didn't like a lot of subjects at school, like maths and science. I just wasn't very good at them, and I hated doing exams and tests and so on.

I Hm. But you were interested in art?

P Yes, I've always enjoyed art.

I So, you left school when you were … ?

P I left school when I was eighteen. I passed my exams – just! – and then I got a job. Then, er, about twenty years later, I decided I wanted to do a degree in art. So I applied to some colleges and I got into the School of Art and Design in Limoges.

I Oh, and how is it?

P It's a great experience, completely different from school.

I How exactly?

P Well, I'm studying something I really want to study, you know?

I Right.

P And I'm a lot older and more confident, so it's easier to ask questions, talk to the teachers, things like that.

3

I Margaret, you're a student at the University of the Third Age?

MARGARET Yes, we call it the U3A.

I U3A. And what is that exactly?

M Well, 'the third age' means it's for people over fifty. Anyone over fifty can join. We have meetings and talks in members' homes, and we don't do exams or get degrees. So, you see, it's not a typical university!

I And why did you join?

M Well, I retired three years ago. I had a lot of free time, and nothing to do. It wasn't a very happy time, to be honest. Then I read something about the U3A and went to a talk and it was great.

I Hm. What kind of courses have you done?

M Oh, there are so many interesting things. I've done courses in music, erm, local history and Spanish. I choose things I haven't studied before.

I And what's next?

M Well, I've never been very good with computers, so, er, last week I signed up for an IT skills course.

■ 1.12

What kind of courses have you done?
I've done courses in music, er, local history and Spanish.
I choose things I haven't studied before.
I've never been very good with computers.

Has she ever studied Spanish?
Yes, she has.
No, she hasn't.

■ 1.13

1 What subjects have you always enjoyed?

2 What subjects have you always been good at?

■ 1.14

3 What's the most useful subject you've ever studied?

4 Who's the best teacher you've ever had?

5 Have you ever done a course in your free time?

6 Have you ever written a thesis or a very long essay?

7 Have you done a lot of exams in your life?

8 What's the most difficult exam you've ever passed?

■ 1.15

INTERVIEWER OK, right. So, it's Lauren, isn't it?

LAUREN Yes, that's right.

I Great. Have you got your form there?

L Yes, here you go.

I And did you bring a copy of your CV?

L Yes.

I OK. Er, let's just have a look. So, you've done lots of different things! Sales … administration … and you've worked in a restaurant.

L Yes, that's right. Last summer.

I OK. And you're looking for work in … ?

L Well, yes, as you can see, I've got experience in sales, administration and catering, so I'm looking for work in any of those areas really.

I Right. Er, let's start with catering. You worked for Café Concerto last summer. What qualifications do you have? Do you have any kind of food safety or hygiene certificate?

L Yes, I've got a certificate in Food Safety for Catering. It's level two.

I Ah, that's excellent. Have you got a copy of that with you?

L Er, no, sorry.

I Oh, that's no problem. Could you fax it over later today? Or bring it in?

L Sure.

I Great. Now, administration … How are you with computers?

L Well, I have experience working with Word and Excel, so quite good, I think.

I OK, good, and more generally ... it doesn't say here, no ... do you have a driving licence?

L Yes, I do.

I Good. And what languages do you speak?

L Erm, a little French and Spanish.

I OK. And more recently you worked in sales for CSP. Did you enjoy that?

L Yes, I've been in sales for a year now and I worked for CSP for six months. It was a nice company.

I So why did you decide to leave?

L Well ... it's quite a small company, you know. I've always wanted to work for a big company. I think that would be a good experience for me.

I OK. Now ... what would you say are your strengths and weaknesses?

L Hm, that's a difficult question. Well, I'm good at talking to people, I think. And I really enjoy working in a team. But maybe I'm not very good at working on my own? I prefer working with people.

I OK, great. Well, I'm sure we'll have something for you. We'll put your details on our system and see what we have. And I'll need to contact your references.

1.16

CLARE Hello, CSP, Clare speaking. How can I help you?

YUSUF Oh, hello, my name's Yusuf Karim. I'm from the job agency, Findajob. Could I speak to Lisa Moore, please?

C Certainly. Can I ask you the reason for the call?

Y Of course. I'm calling about an ex-CSP employee, Lauren Gordon. Lisa Moore was her manager.

C Thank you. Let me just see if Lisa's available. Hello? I'm afraid she's in a meeting. Can I take a message?

Y I'm sorry, this line's not very good. Could you say that again, please?

C Yes, of course, I'm sorry. Would you like me to take a message?

Y Yes, please.

C Er, what was your name again, please?

Y Yes, it's Yusuf Karim.

C Could you spell that for me?

Y Yes, it's Yusuf with a Y, Y-U-S-U-F, and Karim is K-A-R-I-M.

C OK. And what's your telephone number?

Y I'll give you my mobile number. It's oh four one two, double five six, two oh seven.

C Sorry, can you speak more slowly, please?

Y Yes, it's oh four one two, double five six, two oh seven.

C Right. And has Lisa got your email address?

Y Er, no. It's y dot karim at findajob dot com dot au.

C Sorry, y dot karim at ... ?

Y Findajob – that's one word – dot com dot au.

C OK, so that's y dot karim at findajob dot com dot au. And what would you like me to tell her?

Y Well, I'd like to ask her some questions about Lauren Gordon, what was she like as an employee and things. It would be great if she could phone me.

C OK, I'll give her the message and ask her to contact you.

Y Thank you. That's very helpful.

C No problem. Goodbye.

1.17

1 Can you speak more slowly, please?
2 What was your name again, please?
  Could you say that again, please?
  Sorry, y dot karim at ... ?
3 Could you spell that for me?
4 OK.
  Right.
  OK, so that's ...

1.18

lawyer   visitor   grammar   neighbour

1.19

1 dollar   6 colour
2 winter   7 composer
3 computer   8 footballer
4 singer   9 calendar
5 doctor   10 teenager

1.20

unfriendly, friendly
expensive, cheap
relaxing, stressful
inconvenient, convenient
quiet, noisy
boring, interesting
empty, crowded
old-fashioned, modern

1.21

LYNN So, where are you taking me?

BRYAN Well, I've had a look in this guide and, er, I think these three look quite good. Have a look.

L Hmm.

B What do you think?

L Well, they all look nice ... but I went to Bopha Devi recently.

B OK, then, uh, what about this one?

L Abla's?

B Yeah, I've heard the food there's very good.

L I don't know ... it's a long way from here.

B OK, er ... how about The Bridge?

L Yeah, we could sit outside. Ah, but do you think they do vegetarian food?

B I'm sure they do.

L OK, let's go to The Bridge. Is that OK with you?

B Sure, it's your birthday.

L Great.

B I'll call and book a table for, say, seven thirty?

L Fine.

B Right, what's the number?

1.22

WAITER Hi, are you ready to order?

LYNN Yes, I think so. Erm ... what's the soup of the day?

W Er, today it's, er, cream of mushroom soup.

L OK, so I'll have that ... and, er, the pasta, please.

W OK. And for you, sir?

BRYAN Yeah, could I have the cheese salad to start ...

W Cheese salad ...

B ... and then the steak?

W Fine, and how would you like your steak?

B Er, medium, please.

W All right. Can I get you something to drink?

B Do you want some wine?

L Not right now actually, maybe later.

B OK.

L Can we have a bottle of water?

W Sure. Sparkling or still?

L Er, still.

B Yep.

L Still, please.

W OK, thanks very much.

1.23

Can we have a bottle of water?

1.24

1 Could I have the cheese salad to start ... and then the steak?
2 OK, so I'll have that and the pasta, please.
3 Medium, please.
4 Still, please.
5 Yes, I think so. What's the soup of the day?

1.25

1 I'd like to book a table for two, please.
2 My parents cook a big meal for nine or ten people every weekend.
3 Could I have the chicken in garlic sauce, please?
4 That table in the corner's free. Why don't we sit there?
5 Would you like a bottle of water with your meal?
6 The weather was great, so we sat at a table on the terrace.
7 There's a good menu with lots of vegetarian dishes and the staff are very friendly.
8 I'll have the salmon with rice, please.

1.26

MANUEL So how about we organise a barbecue?

EREN Barbecues can be tricky because that means that we have to cook meat and quite a few people are vegetarian.

M Mmm. That's a thought.

SARAH We could do some pasta alternative, maybe?

SUSANNE No, we can put veggies on the barbecue as well.

E Yeah, that could be ... but then some people are really strict that they don't want, like, any kind of meat, fat and stuff being mixed with ...

SA Yes, that's true as well.

M But we could have a barbie, we could have like mushrooms and things like this on one burner and another ... and meat and sausages on another place.

SU Separated, yeah.

E I think that would work if you have like, yeah ...

M Different grills.

E Yes, that would work.

M So what should we buy?

E Well, sausages are nice.

1.27

MANUEL What about salads?

EREN Greek salad I can do.

M Okay, okay. We need to buy some feta cheese then.

E Yeah, feta cheese and some black olives and, erm, olive oil.

M Very important. What about dessert?

SUSANNE Now this is getting too much now.

M Well, it depends. A lot of people are going to come.

SU Well, then keep it easy and simple. Ice cream?

M What about fruit? Melons?

1.28

MATT Well, in my family we usually eat together in the evening, erm, maybe pasta, salad, chicken. Everyone sits around the table and eats and talks about everything – what we did that day, how we feel ... erm, our plans for the next day, the food ... whatever. I don't know what other people do but I send my kids to wash their hands before dinner. Er, Friday evenings are a bit more relaxed. If we're at home, we usually have a quick meal in front of the TV ... pizza or Chinese food or something. No one really talks. Everyone's a bit tired by Friday.

CARLOS Er, in my family we all have breakfast at different times because we all get up at different times. Later in the day, if we have guests, we usually have a ... you know, a buffet-style dinner ... and everyone chooses things from a side table and then takes their food to the main table. My mum says *bon appétit* before we start eating but that's all. And during the meal, we talk about work and family and football and different things but we don't usually talk about the food.

1.29

enjoy   employee   noisy   boil

1.30

1 oil
2 join
3 self-employed
4 appointment
5 toilet
6 boyfriend
7 employ
8 choice

1.31

A meter
B fare
C receipt
D passenger
E taxi rank
F change

1.32

1

NICOLA Hi. Er, how much is it to the city centre?

TONY Er, that depends on the traffic. It's usually about thirty, thirty-five dollars.

N OK. Can I put my case in the back?

T I'll do that for you. So, where are we headed?

N Erm, can you take me to the Park Inn?

T The Park Inn on Broadway, right?

N Um, yes, that's the one.

T All right ... So, is this your first time in Canada?

N Well, no. I came here with my parents, like, fifteen years ago but I don't remember much.

T Right, so what brings you back here?

T Here we are. The Park Inn.

N Thanks. Er, how much is it?

T Thirty-one fifty, please.

N Just make it thirty-five dollars.

T Thanks very much ... And here's your change, fifteen dollars.

N OK. Thanks.

T Now, let's get your case.

2

DAN Hello. The Royal Bank on Howe Street, please.

TONY OK.

T OK, that'll be eight dollars and fifty cents.

D Actually, could you wait here for five minutes? I just have to get some papers.

T Well, OK, but can you pay me first?

D Of course ... here's ten. I'll be back in five minutes.

T OK.

D Thanks for waiting. OK, I'd like to go to the airport, please.

T OK. Which terminal?

D Domestic, please.

T All right, the domestic terminal ... So you're going somewhere on business, right?

D Yeah, I've got some meetings in Calgary.

T So do you work for the bank?

T OK, that's thirty-five dollars and 75 cents.

D And can I have a receipt, please?

T Sure ... here you are. Have a safe trip now.

D Thanks, bye.

1.33

1 How much is it to the city centre?
2 Can you take me to the Park Inn?
3 I'd like to go to the airport, please.
4 Can I put my case in the back?
5 And can I have a receipt, please?

1.34

What was he doing?
He was standing outside the terminal.
He wasn't looking very happy.

Were they going back to Canada?
Yes, they were.
No, they weren't.

1.35

The Ten-Dollar Bill
One sunny morning a man was walking through the city on his way to work. He was wearing a smart suit and tie and talking on his phone. Suddenly, the sun went in and it started raining heavily. The man saw a taxi and started running towards it. As he was running, a ten-dollar bill fell from his pocket onto the ground, but he didn't notice. He got into the cab, shut the door, and the cab drove away.

1.36

OSMAN Well, er, I was travelling to the USA on business and, uh, I got a plane from Germany, from Frankfurt. Anyway I was just reading the airline magazine and relaxing, when suddenly some late passengers arrived. A few of them came into Business Class, where I was sitting. One of them was this really big guy with a huge beard and sunglasses. He was wearing a black biker jacket, black leather trousers and he had a lot of tattoos. He looked kind of scary, actually. Anyway, he sat down next to me and before I could pretend to fall asleep, he introduced himself and we had a good chat. He was a nice guy. Interesting. His name was Bernd, I think, but it was a long time ago. Then, recently, I was in Germany again and, er, I turned on the television and there he was, on a news programme. He's a top manager for the Harley-Davidson clothing company in Germany, and he was speaking at some big conference. And he was still wearing his biker clothes, so I recognised him immediately.

ANNIE I went to Montpellier, er, one or two years ago. I was looking for a little restaurant to eat on my own. It was in February but in Montpellier it was really nice weather so you could eat outside. So I sat at a table for two. At one point a man arrived and there was only one table for five available, so he asked me if he could sit at my table, erm, and we started having a chat. He was a really nice person. He was from Switzerland and he was studying, er, French, erm, in Montpellier, so I started teaching him a bit. We met several times when I was there and, erm, next to Montpellier there is a nice town, next to the sea, erm, so we, we had a day trip there and, and that's it really. We became pen friends but of course I have my boyfriend at home so, erm, that's it.

1.37

ASTRID   When I was learning French, once I knew a few basic words, I liked reading children's books. I found it very useful, because the sentences are very simple.

TOM   When I was learning German, I used to change the language on my computer games to German. Then I could pretend to my parents that I was learning, instead of playing. But it really did help me learn.

MASHA   When I learn a foreign language, I like watching DVDs in that language, er, with subtitles on so I can, er, pause and look in a dictionary what the word means and see how it's spelt. And also when I was in Germany learning German I changed the menu of my mobile phone into German, so that helped.

1.38

VALÉRIE   Good morning, can you take me to the Holiday Inn, please?

TONY   Sure. Which one?

v   Er, the one on Broadway, please.

T   So, what brings you to Vancouver?

v   I have some old friends here. Actually, we were at university together.

T   So it's not your first time here?

v   Oh, no. I visit every three or four months.

T   Right. So you like it here?

v   Yes. In fact, I'd really like to live here.

T   Oh, yeah? Where do you live?

v   In Montreal. Well, actually, I've got a small business there.

T   Really? What do you do?

v   I own a couple of restaurants.

1.39

right	neighbours
night	bought
frightening	through
eight	straight

1.40

enough   laugh   yoghurt   spaghetti

1.41

1	light	6	flight
2	thought	7	spaghetti
3	eighteen	8	daughter
4	neighbourhood	9	frightening
5	enough	10	tonight

2.1

A	a cash machine	D	notes
B	bills	E	coins
C	cash	F	a card

2.2

THIAGO   Hello. Do you have Scottish pounds?

ASSISTANT   Er, no, we don't, but English pounds are OK in Scotland.

T   Oh, OK. Can I change these euros, please?

A   Of course. That's fifty, a hundred, and fifty, sixty, seventy, eighty. That's a hundred and eighty euros, yes?

T   Yes, that's right.

A   Right, that's ... a hundred and fifty pounds. Here you are.

T   Sorry, do you have any smaller notes?

A   No problem. Are twenties OK?

T   That's great, thanks.

2.3

1

ASSISTANT   Hello, can I help?

THIAGO   Yes, I'll take these postcards, please.

A   OK.

T   And, er, do you have any maps?

A   I'm sorry, we don't have any maps at the moment. You could try next door.

T   OK.

A   Anything else?

T   No, that's all, thanks. How much is that?

A   Eight postcards. That comes to six pounds forty, please.

T   Can I pay by card?

A   I'm afraid not, no. There's a cash machine just around—

T   No, it's OK, I've got some cash, I think.

A   Thank you. And that's 60 pence change.

T   Thanks.

A   Would you like a bag?

T   Er, yes, please.

A   There you are. Bye now.

T   Goodbye.

2

WAITRESS   How was your meal? Everything OK?

THIAGO   It was very nice, thank you.

W   Would you like to see the dessert menu?

T   No, thanks.

W   Maybe some coffee?

T   Er, no, that's OK. Could I have the bill?

W   Certainly. How would you like to pay?

T   Do you take cards?

W   Yes, of course. Just one moment.

W   Can you type in your PIN and press 'ENTER', please.

T   Er, right.

W   And there's your receipt. Thanks very much.

T   Thanks.

3

ASSISTANT   Good morning.

THIAGO   Hi. One student, please.

A   Can I see your student card?

T   Sure. Here you are.

A   That's fine. That's two fifty, please.

T   OK.

A   Sorry, do you have anything smaller?

T   I'm sorry, no, that's all I've got.

A   That's OK. That's three, four, five, ten, thirty, fifty pounds. And here's your ticket and a guide to the museum exhibits.

T   Thanks very much.

2.4

1   Anything else?

2   How much is that?

3   Can I pay by card?

4   Would you like a bag?

5   Could I have the bill?

6   How would you like to pay?

7   Do you take cards?

8   Can I see your student card?

9   Do you have anything smaller?

2.5

1   Grameen's customers have to make groups of five people.

2   They don't have to be women.

3   They can't usually get credit from normal banks.

4   They can get bigger loans if they make all their repayments.

2.6

MEGAN   When you go over to someone's house for dinner in Canada, you should probably ask ahead of time if you can bring something with you, just to be nice. Erm, and you should probably show up with a gift. Maybe you can bring a bottle of wine, or maybe some flowers, something like that. The other thing to remember is that you have to take your shoes off when you get to the house. Don't wear your shoes inside.

YUKIO   OK, when you go to a Japanese hot spring, there are a few rules. Women go to the women's area and men to the men's area. First, you go into the washing room. Here you wash yourself with a towel and lots of soap. Then you have to wash off all the soap so you are really clean. After that, you can get into the hot spring. The water's quite hot, so you shouldn't stay in it too long. You can get out and rest for a while and then go back in. What else? Well, you can't make a lot of noise. The spring should be a quiet place where people can just relax.

2.7

1

A   When can we meet? Tomorrow? Sunday?

B   It doesn't really matter. I'm free all weekend.

2

A   I'm sorry I'm late! Where's the meeting?

B Don't worry about it. The meeting hasn't started yet.

3
A Do you like parties?
B It depends. Generally yes, but not when there are too many people.

4
A Do you want to come to the cinema tonight?
B Mm, I'm not sure I have time. I'll think about it, OK?

5
A Have we got any food at home?
B Not really ... we've got some milk in the fridge. That's it.

6
A What time do I have to start work?
B It's up to you. But you have to be here eight hours a day.

2.8

JOHN What do you think about this article? I think I agree. You shouldn't tell people how much you earn.

HAYLEY Why not? I tell people how much I earn!

J Really?

H Yeah, sure. Why not?

J It just seems really ... I don't know.

H I mean, I don't tell people when I first meet them. I don't say, 'Hi, my name's Hayley and I earn fifty thousand dollars a year.' But if it's part of the conversation, then, sure. It's part of my life, it's part of who I am.

J Really? In the UK, in general, I don't think people like to say how much they earn. It's just more private, maybe.

2.9

conversation   expression   musician

2.10

1 education	6 action
2 discussion	7 electrician
3 information	8 promotion
4 expression	9 organisation
5 politician	10 introduction

2.11

1 How many books do you have at home?
2 How many hours a week do you work or study?
3 How many emails do you get every day?
4 How many cups of coffee or tea do you drink a day?
5 How many kilometres do you drive in a typical month?
6 How many minutes does it take you to get to this class?
7 How many times have you travelled by aeroplane?
8 How many people live in your home town?

2.12

A doing the vacuuming
B cleaning the windows
C doing the dusting
D doing the ironing

E doing the cooking
F making the bed

2.13

JEEVAN The summer months in India can actually be quite dangerous; it's so hot before the rains come. The most important thing is to drink a lot, to cover up when you go outside, to cover your head. You'll see Indian men and women wearing long clothes which cover everything, including their arms and legs. Only tourists wear shorts and T-shirts in the hot sun. On summer afternoons in Kolkata, where I live, the streets are empty because it's too hot to go out, so most people are either at work or at home, asleep. A lot of people use air conditioning but it's expensive. Not everyone can afford it. Cold drinks like *mango panna* are really popular. This is a drink made from unripe mangoes; it really helps to cool your body.

VASILY I live in Moscow, in Russia. Our winters last from, er, about November to March and we get quite a lot of snow. In January and February, it's usually minus five to minus ten degrees Celsius but it can get a lot colder, even down to minus thirty. OK, maybe it isn't as cold as Siberia, but it's cold enough! You have to wear lots of big, heavy clothes and boots and, er, everything takes longer ... putting clothes on to go out, taking them off when you get inside. And you have to be more careful on the roads too because they can be icy. Everyone has to carry an emergency kit in the car, so if the car stops you'll be OK. These days a lot of young people prefer to escape the winter and go to much hotter countries like Egypt and Turkey; but most people I know spend half the winter at home watching TV. Me? I like to get out of the city and go skiing. But I think we all look forward to the New Year celebrations, which are really fun and help us to get through our long winters.

2.14

You have to be more careful on the roads.
That's hotter than the surface of the sun.
The heaviest hailstone fell in Bangladesh in 1986.
The most important thing is to drink a lot.
It weighed one kilogram and was as large as a melon.
It isn't as cold as Siberia.

2.15

INTERVIEWER Excuse me, do you have a few minutes?

SALLY Well ...

I We're opening a new fitness centre and we'd like to find out what local

people really need. Could I ask you some questions? We'd really value your opinion.

s Er, yes, OK.

I Thank you. It'll only take a few minutes.

s No problem.

I Right. So, erm, do you use a fitness centre at the moment?

s Er, yes, sometimes.

I Where is that, if you don't mind me asking?

s That's OK, I go to the Meanwood Fitness Centre in Kent Town.

I Right, and what do you think of it?

s Well, to be honest, it's not that good.

I Yes? Why is that?

s Well, the pool's OK, but it could be bigger. And there should be time for adults only. I'd prefer women-only classes as well.

I OK, I'll make a note of that. Ah, what about the facilities?

s Well, the facilities could definitely be better too. I don't mind the changing rooms but I'd much rather have private showers.

I Private showers. Right. Now, we're planning to have a sauna. Are you interested in using a sauna?

s Er, well, maybe. But I think I'd rather have a nicer pool than a sauna.

I OK. Erm, how often do you go to the fitness centre?

s Well, I try to go once a week, but I'd like to go more often.

I Uh-huh. And how long do you usually spend there?

s Erm, about an hour and a half, I suppose. I usually swim for half an hour, then go to the gym for a bit.

I OK. And which machines do you prefer using in the gym?

s Well, I generally use the running and rowing machines.

2.16

1 h free	5 g hair
2 c shopping	6 f energy
3 d current	7 b stay
4 e best	8 a her

2.17

1 gym	6 cleaning
2 thunderstorm	7 rainbow
3 cycling	8 vacuuming
4 chores	9 tornado
5 clouds	10 working

2.18

1

BILL Would you mind answering a few questions, please? It won't take long.

SHEILA Er, yes, that's OK.

B Thank you. Are you happy with the fitness centre generally?

s Erm, well, it could be better.

B Oh. I see. Do you think you could tell me a bit more?

s Well, to be honest, the pool isn't always very clean. And the staff don't seem very interested.

B Oh dear. Well, I'll definitely tell the manager.

2

BEN Hi. I wonder if you could change this ten for me. I need some coins for the ticket machine.

CLODAGH Sorry, but I'd rather not. People are always asking me for change.

B Oh.

C Perhaps you'd like to buy something?

B Erm, no, not really.

3

PHIL Here's your drink. Sorry it took so long.

CATHERINE So, what do you think of the game?

P Erm, it's a bit boring.

C Boring?

P Well, you know I'm not really interested in football.

C So should we go? The second half starts in two minutes.

P No, you stay here. I'll do some shopping, then come back in an hour, OK?

C Well, OK. See you later.

2.19

1 Can you answer a few questions? Would you mind answering a few questions, please?

2 Can you change this ten for me? I wonder if you could change this ten for me.

3 Can you tell me a bit more? Do you think you could tell me a bit more?

4 No, I don't want to. Sorry, but I'd rather not.

5 No, I don't need anything. No, not really.

6 The pool is dirty. The pool isn't always very clean.

7 The staff aren't interested. The staff don't seem very interested.

8 It's boring. It's a bit boring.

9 I'm not interested in football. I'm not really interested in football.

2.20

SUE Yes?

ANDRE It's André. I want to talk to Sue.

s This is Sue, but I'm busy. Call me later.

A Tomorrow?

s No. I don't work on Sundays.

A Monday afternoon?

s OK. Call me at the office. The mobile's expensive.

A OK. Bye.

2.21

comfortable available possible sensible

2.22

1 fashionable   6 sensible
2 memorable   7 enjoyable
3 available   8 comfortable
4 terrible   9 horrible
5 possible   10 impossible

2.23

TOURIST OFFICER Can I help you?

LIZZY Oh, yes, please. How can I get to Anne Frank's house?

T Oh, you can walk from here. It's very easy. Let me show you on the map.

L OK.

T We're next to the main train station.

L Yeah.

T Go out of here and turn left. Go down the big street. It's called Damrak.

L OK.

T You'll go past a big building on your left, the Beurs.

L OK.

T If you continue along Damrak, you'll come to the Dam.

L That's the big square, right?

T That's right. You'll see the National Monument on your left, and the Royal Palace on your right.

L Right.

T So, turn right and go past the palace. Then go along Raadhuisstraat, here, for about five hundred metres.

L OK.

T When you get to the canal called Prinsengracht, turn right. The house is by the canal, just here.

L That sounds pretty easy. Is it far?

T No, two kilometres, maybe a bit less. It's a nice walk.

L That's great. Thanks for all your help.

T You're welcome. Is there anything else I can help you with?

L No thanks, that's fine.

2.24

Go out of here and turn left.

2.25

1 Turn right and go past the palace.

2 You'll go past a big building on your left, the Beurs.

3 You'll see the National Monument on your left and the Royal Palace on your right.

2.26

TOURIST OFFICER Hello, can I help you?

SERGEI Yes. Erm, I've only got one free day to see the sights in Amsterdam, and I was wondering, do you organise tours of the city?

T Er, yeah, we can, but it's quite easy to get around the city on your own.

s OK.

T But, erm, you've only got one day? That's not enough!

s Yes, I know, I have to leave first thing tomorrow, so …

T OK, well, er, what would you like to do?

s Erm, I don't know. Have you got a map or something?

T Yes, we have. Here you are. Er, it has all the sights on it …

s Ah. Thanks. Can you recommend some things to see?

T Well, one of the most popular things to see is Anne Frank's house. That's here.

s Ah, of course. I've heard of her.

T Yes, this is the house where she wrote the famous diary. Erm, there are often long queues, unfortunately, so the best time to go is early evening.

s Well, that should be OK. It sounds interesting.

T Yes, if you're interested in history, it's definitely a good place to visit. OK, er, we have a lot of museums. So, if you like art, there's the Van Gogh museum here.

s Ah, right. Er, do you sell tickets?

T I'm afraid we don't, no. Er, there's also a science museum – NEMO. That's here.

s Hm, maybe not this time, but the Van Gogh museum sounds good. Erm … what about this? I don't know how to say it. The Gardens?

T Ah, yes, The Keukenhof Gardens. They're very nice but they're not actually in Amsterdam.

s Ah.

T You have to get a train and then a bus, it takes about an hour.

s Hm, OK. I think that's too far.

T Right, what else? Erm …

s Actually, I think that's, er, probably enough. Thanks very much.

T No problem. Have a nice day.

s Thanks.

2.27

A Rob! Can you answer the door? I'm doing the washing up.

B Yeah, OK. Who is it?

A It'll be Leona. I invited her for a coffee.

A Don't forget, it's Deiter's birthday on Monday.

B Ah, yes. How old is he?

A He'll be twenty-five, I think.

2.28

1

A I'll have the pasta, please.

B Fine. And would you like something to drink?

2

A Are you OK? You don't look well.

B Hm, it's very hot in here!

3

A Hello?

B Hi, Jan. It's Laurence.

A Sorry, I can't talk now. I'm in a meeting.

2.29

NATALIE When I go travelling, which I really like to do a lot, I think it's very important to try to speak the language of the people of the country you're visiting. I think it's a good way of getting to know people and understanding a bit more.

PAULA Yeah, but sometimes don't you think that makes conversation a bit slow, like if you're walking around with a little dictionary and you have to sort of look up words every time you want to say something and if the other person speaks your language then maybe it's just easier to, you know, speak the language that you both share.

N Yeah, I think you're right in that way. I know when I go to France even if I speak French the people reply to me in English because I don't speak French well enough, but I think it's wrong to go to a country and expect people to speak to you in your language. I think if they are willing, then it's OK.

P Yeah, probably. You're probably right, yeah.

2.30

OK, you go out of here and turn left and you'll see a coffee machine in the corner. Turn right and continue along the corridor. Turn right again and pass the teachers' room. The room you want is on your right, after the library.

2.31

build   buy   fruit

2.32

1 biscuit	6 fruit
2 build	7 guide
3 buy	8 guy
4 guitar	9 juice
5 suit	

Vowels

Short vowels

/ə/	/æ/	/ʊ/	/ɒ/	/ɪ/	/i/	/e/	/ʌ/
teach<u>er</u> <u>a</u>go	m<u>a</u>rried <u>am</u>	b<u>oo</u>k c<u>ou</u>ld	<u>on</u> g<u>o</u>t	<u>in</u> sw<u>i</u>m	happ<u>y</u> eas<u>y</u>	w<u>e</u>t <u>a</u>ny	c<u>u</u>p <u>u</u>nder

Long vowels

/ɜː/	/ɑː/	/uː/	/ɔː/	/iː/
h<u>er</u> sh<u>ir</u>t	<u>ar</u>m c<u>ar</u>	bl<u>ue</u> t<u>oo</u>	<u>or</u> w<u>a</u>lk	<u>ea</u>t m<u>ee</u>t

Dipthongs

/eə/	/ɪə/	/ʊə/	/ɔɪ/	/aɪ/	/eɪ/	/əʊ/	/aʊ/
ch<u>air</u> wh<u>ere</u>	n<u>ear</u> w<u>e're</u>	t<u>our</u>	b<u>oy</u> n<u>oi</u>sy	n<u>i</u>ne <u>eye</u>	<u>eigh</u>t d<u>ay</u>	g<u>o</u> <u>o</u>ver	<u>ou</u>t br<u>ow</u>n

Consonants voiced unvoiced

/b/	/ð/	/v/	/dʒ/	/d/	/z/	/g/	/ʒ/
<u>b</u>e <u>b</u>it	mo<u>th</u>er <u>th</u>e	<u>v</u>ery li<u>v</u>e	<u>j</u>ob pa<u>g</u>e	<u>d</u>own re<u>d</u>	maga<u>z</u>ine	<u>g</u>irl ba<u>g</u>	televi<u>s</u>ion
/p/	/θ/	/f/	/tʃ/	/t/	/s/	/k/	/ʃ/
<u>p</u>ark sho<u>p</u>	<u>th</u>ink bo<u>th</u>	<u>f</u>ace lau<u>gh</u>	<u>ch</u>ips tea<u>ch</u>	<u>t</u>ime whi<u>t</u>e	<u>s</u>ee ri<u>c</u>e	<u>c</u>old loo<u>k</u>	<u>sh</u>oe fi<u>sh</u>
/m/	/n/	/ŋ/	/l/	/r/	/w/	/j/	/h/
<u>m</u>e na<u>m</u>e	<u>n</u>ow rai<u>n</u>	thi<u>ng</u> dri<u>nk</u>	<u>l</u>ate hel<u>lo</u>	ca<u>rr</u>y <u>wr</u>ite	<u>w</u>e <u>wh</u>ite	<u>y</u>ou <u>y</u>es	<u>h</u>ot <u>h</u>and

Irregular verbs

Infinitive	Past simple	Part participle
All forms are the same		
		bet
		cost
		cut
		hit
		let
		put
		set

Past simple and past participle are the same	
bring	brought
build	built
burn	burned
buy	bought
catch	caught
feed	fed
feel	felt
fight	fought
find	found
get	got
have	had
hear	heard
hold	held
keep	kept
leave	left
lend	lent
lose	lost
make	made
mean	meant
meet	met
pay	paid
read /riːd/	read /red/
say	said
sell	sold
send	sent
shoot	shot
sit	sat
sleep	slept
spend	spent
stand	stood
teach	taught
tell	told
think	thought
understand	understood
win	won

Infinitive	Past simple	Past participle
All forms are different		
be	was / were	been
begin	began	begun
blow	blew	blown
break	broke	broken
can	could	been able to
choose	chose	chosen
do	did	done
draw	drew	drawn
drink	drank	drunk
drive	drove	driven
eat	ate	eaten
fall	fall	fallen
fly	flew	flown
forget	forgot	forgotten
freeze	froze	frozen
give	gave	given
go	went	been / gone
grow	grew	grown
hide	hid	hidden
know	knew	known
ride	rode	ridden
ring	rang	rung
rise	rose	risen
see	saw	seen
shake	shook	shaken
show	showed	shown
sing	sang	sung
speak	spoke	spoken
steal	stole	stolen
swim	swam	swum
take	took	taken
throw	threw	thrown
wake	woke	woken
wear	wore	worn
write	wrote	written
Infinitive and past participle are the same		
become	became	become
come	came	come
run	ran	run
Infinitive and past simple are the same		
	beat	beaten

English Unlimited

B1 Pre-intermediate A
Self-study Pack (Workbook)

Maggie Baigent, Chris Cavey & Nick Robinson

CAMBRIDGE
UNIVERSITY PRESS

Acknowledgements

The authors would like to thank the editorial team in Cambridge, particularly Greg Sibley and Neil Holloway. Many thanks also to Catriona Watson-Brown for her ever-thorough copy-editing.

Maggie Baigent would like to thank Michael Cotton for his loyalty and support.

Chris Cavey would like to thank Kate, Lily and Ella for their patience and support.

Nick Robinson would like to thank Anna Barnard.

The authors and publishers are also grateful to the following contributors:

Text design and page make-up: Stephanie White at Kamae Design
Picture research: Hilary Luckcock

The authors and publishers acknowledge the following sources of copyright material and are grateful for the permissions granted. While every effort has been made, it has not always been possible to identify the sources of all the material used, or to trace all copyright holders. If any omissions are brought to our notice, we will be happy to include the appropriate acknowledgements on reprinting.

For the text on p. 7: © Copyright University of Glamorgan 2008–2009. All rights reserved; for the text on p. 27: Reproduced with permission from the Lonely Planet Website www.lonelyplanet.com © 2009 Lonely Planet Publications Pty Ltd; for the text on p. 37: © Simon Calder, the *Independent*, 2nd August 2008.

The publisher has used its best endeavours to ensure that the URLs for external websites referred to in this book are correct and active at the time of going to press. However, the publisher has no responsibility for the websites and can make no guarantee that a site will remain live or that the content is or will remain appropriate.

The publishers are grateful to the following for the permissions to reproduce copyright photographs and material:

Key: l = left, c = centre, r = right, t = top, b = bottom

Alamy/©ImageState for p4(tc), /©SuperStock for p4(bc), /©Alex Segre for p4(c), /©blickwinkel for p11(r), /©Elizabeth Whiting & Associates for p14(t), /©imagebroker for p16(8), /©i love images for p17(l), /©PhotosIndia.com LLC for p17(c), /©Emilio Ereza for p20, /©Blend Images for p21(tl), /©Image Source Black for p21(tr), /©Diffused Productions for p21(bl), /©Chris Rout for p21(br), /©Shoosmith Railway Collection for p24(l), /©imagebroker for p24(c), /©Derek Askill for p25(t), /©Leslie Garland Picture Library for p32, /©Frank Chmura for p36, /©International Photobank for p37, /©Vintage Image for p41(c), /©Adrian Sherratt for p57, /©Jon Arnold Images for p59(br), /©Phil Degginger for p59(tr), /©Hola Images for p61(tcr), /©Peter Arnold Inc for p61(bc), /©David J Green-Lifestyle for p65(b), /©John Miller for p69(cl); Corbis/©Bernardo Bucci for p10(l), /©Turbo for p40(b), /©flame for p44(7), /©Eric Cahan for p52(t), /©Barry Rosenthal for p55(t), /©Image Source for p69(tl), /©Shawn Frederick for p69(b); Fears and Kahn for 40(tl, tc, tr); Getty Images/©Win-Initiative for p11(l), /©Photographer's Choice for p41(t), /©PhotoDisc for p44(1), /©Hulton Archive for p61(t), /©Hisham Ibrahim for p61(cl), /©Charlie Schuck for p69(tr), /©Simon Watson for p70; istockphoto/©Stephanie Swartz for p9(2), /©Brad Wieland for p9(3), /©Dawn Liljenquist for p9(4), /©Radu Razvan for p9(5), /©Amanda Krishnan for p21(bc), /©Tom Hahn for p25(b), /©Steve Geer for p45, /©Simone van den Berg for p46(t), /©mamahoohooba for p46(ct), /©Liza McCorkie for p46(cb), /©TommL for p46(b), /©Ana Vasileva for p51(b), /©Thorsten Rust for p54(b), /©Linda & Colin McKie for p59(bl), /©Juergen Bosse for p60(t), /©ad_doward for p61(cr); Lebrecht Music & Arts/©Martin Thompson for p4(tr), 4(br); Masterfile/©Chad Johnston for p10(r); Photolibrary/©Thinkstock for p9(1), /©Joel Sartore for p11(c), /©Comstock for p15, /©fancy for p17(r), /©Sylvain Grandadam for p19, /©Olive Images for p24(r), /©Digital Vision for p44(2), /©Digital Vision for p44(5), /©Digital Vision for p44(6), /©White for p44(8), /©Thinkstock for p49, /©Blend Images for p51(t), /©Liat Chen for p55(b), /©Jeff Greenberg for p65(t); Pictures Colour Library/©George Munday for p4(br), /©Intervision Ltd for p14(b); Punchstock/©Digital Vision for p14(l), /©Cultura for p31; Rex Features/©Ben Alcraft for p39, /©Sipa Press / Rex Features for p60(b); Shutterstock/©Timurpix for p4(tl), /©Ales Nowak for p6, /©Phil Date for p9(6), /©Karin Lau for p9(7), /©gpalmer for p9(8), /©ZTS for p16(1), /©vinicius Tupinamba for p16(2), /©luchschen for p16(3), /©Kentoh for p16(4), /©Anton Gvozdikov for p16(5), /©Chin Kit Sen for p16(6), /©Juha-Pekka Kervinen for p16(7), /©stoupa for p16(9), /©Robert Redelowski for p16(10), /©iNNOCENt for p18(tr), /©Aki Jinn for p18(br), /©Johnathan Esper for p33, /©Galyna Andrushko for p44(3), /©Photosani for p44(4), /©Chepko Danil Vitarevich for p52(b), /©Pichugin Dmitry for p59(tl), /©yurok for p59(tc), /©Juriah Mosin for p61(cc), /©Jeff Gynane for p61(br), /©Shi Yali for p61(bl), /©ene for p64(tl), /©Jaroslaw Grudzvinski for p64(tr), /©Chunni4691 for p64(br), /©Planner for p64(tc), /©Jessmine for p64(bl), /©Eric Gevaert for p68(bl), /©VeF for p68(bc), /©objectsforall for p68(br), /©Otmar Smit for p69(cr), /©Soundsnaps for p73(r), /©Mark William Richardson for p73(l).

Illustrations by Tom Croft, Mark Duffin, Kamae Design, Julian Mosedale, Nigel Sanderson, Martin Sanders

Contents

1 Play

1 Complete the words for different types of music.

Bonneville Music Festival
Music for everyone!

a p _o_ _p_

b c _ _ l _ p s _

c s _ _ _ s _

d h _ p - _ _ p

e r _ g g _ _ _

f c l a _ _ _ _ _ _ _ _ music

g f _ _ _ k music

2 Circle the correct words to complete what the people in the festival say about music.

1 We have a special instrument called / is the steel drum. _b_

2 I was learned / brought up to play / sing classical music, but now I play guitar and sing in a band.

3 Our traditional / classical music is called folk.

4 I learned how / what to play the violin when I was little.

5 It's similar to / of a lot of music from Cuba; in fact, it's a mixture of Cuban and Puerto Rican dance music.

3 Match the sentences in Exercise 2 to the correct photos in Exercise 1.

Saturday 25th

**18.00
Rumberos de Cuba**
Dance music from Cuba

**19.00
Rachid Taha**
Rock with traditional Algerian rai influence

**20.00
Children of Khmer**
Classical Cambodian dance

**21.00
Sharon Shannon Big Band**
All-star ceilidh (traditional Irish dance)

**22.00
Mor Karbasi**
15th-century songs from Spain by this young female singer

4 Complete the conversation using the expressions in the box.

> have a look   Hang on   idea   not really into   see if
> sounds   that looks   think about   ~~want to~~

CONN I was thinking about going to the festival on Saturday. **Do you** ¹ _want to_ **go?**

RITA It depends what's on. **Why don't we** ² _____ at the programme?

CONN OK. ³ _____ **a minute**. Right, **what do you** ⁴ _____ this – Children of Khmer?

RITA Hm, I'm ⁵ _____ dance. What about Rachid Taha?

CONN The Algerian music? Yes, ⁶ _____ **interesting**.

RITA And the ceilidh ⁷ _____ **good**, too.

CONN Yeah. **So do you want me to** ⁸ _____ there are any tickets?

RITA **Good** ⁹ _____ .

5 Look at the pictures and complete the words.

1 r u n n ing

2 s k _ ing

3 y _ _ _

4 v _ _ _ _ _ _ b a l l

5 h _ _ _ _ _ _

6 k _ _ _ _ _

7 a e _ _ _ _ _ _

8 s w _ _ _ i n g

Over to you

Which sports do you like doing? Write three sentences.

6 Cross out the words that do *not* go with the verbs in bold.

1 **I play** football / hockey / tennis / karate.
2 **I do** yoga / aerobics / skiing / karate.
3 **I go** swimming / skiing / boxing / running.

7 Read the introduction to the article and answer these questions.

1 Where did Wally work?   2 What does he do now?

8 Read the rest of the article quickly. What kind of music does Wally like?

An interview with Wally Cotgrave

Wally Cotgrave is 70 this year. He spent his working life in heavy industrial sites and petro-chemical plants. Then, at the age of 50, he decided to become a singer.

Interviewer Wally, were you always interested in music?

Wally Well, when I was a child, I loved all the Hollywood musicals, and I learned all the songs by watching the films again and again.

Interviewer But how did you get into singing seriously?

Wally Well, I was a terrible singer! People always told me to stop, but I couldn't – I just loved singing. Then, when I was about 50, we moved out of London to a small town with a very active musical group.

I wanted to sing with them, so I had lessons with a brilliant teacher.

Interviewer What kind of music do you sing?

Wally I love all the songs of the 1940s and '50s, but I mostly sing in musicals with the local group.

Interviewer How many shows have you been in?

Wally Oh, too many to remember! But I had solo parts in *Oliver!* and *My Fair Lady*. And I was on TV once for about ten seconds in a talent show!

Interviewer So, how often do you sing these days?

Wally Every day!

Interviewer And are you working on anything special at the moment?

Wally Well, the next show is *Hello, Dolly!*, and there's a solo part for an older man, so I'm preparing for that. I hope I get it!

Interviewer What would you say to someone who wants to sing?

Wally If I can do it, everybody can!

9 Complete the questions about Wally using the verbs in brackets in the correct form. Use the present simple, past simple or present progressive.

1 How __did__ Wally ____learn____ songs when he was young? (learn)

2 _____ he _____ a good voice when he was younger? (have)

3 Why _____ he _____ to have singing lessons? (decide)

4 What kind of music _____ Wally _____? (sing)

5 Who _____ he usually _____ with? (sing)

6 _____ Wally _____ every day? (sing)

7 What _____ he _____ at the moment? (do)

10 Read the article again and write the answers to the questions in Exercise 9.

TimeOut

11 Read these sentences about strange sports. Are they true or false?

1 Octopush is the sport of underwater hockey.   TRUE / FALSE
2 If you zorb, you go down a hill inside a giant ball.   TRUE / FALSE
3 In disc golf, the players throw CDs into a basket.   TRUE / FALSE
4 Chessboxing is a combination of chess and boxing.   TRUE / FALSE
5 In korfball, the players try to put a ball in a *korf*. TRUE / FALSE

12 Which sports sound the most interesting to you? Tick the ones you would like to try.

EXPLORE Reading

13 Look at the web page for the Summer School and write the questions (1–6) in the correct spaces (a–f).

1 What about the social life?
2 ~~What is the Glamorgan Summer School?~~
3 Is there any accommodation?

4 What about off-campus?
5 What courses are on offer?
6 Who can come?

14 Are the sentences true or false?

1 There is good public transport to the university campus.   (TRUE)/ FALSE
2 At the end of every course, you get a qualification.   TRUE / FALSE
3 There are a lot of things to do in Cardiff.   TRUE / FALSE
4 There is no accommodation on campus.   TRUE / FALSE

15 (Circle) the correct meaning of the underlined expressions on the web page. Guess if you are not sure.

1 a it's very expensive
  (b it's not very expensive)
2 a people who like walking
  b people with different experience
3 a people with children can go to the Summer School
  b people with children can go to the sports camp
4 a there are a lot of different courses
  b you can only find these courses on the Summer School
5 a there are a lot of different types of entertainment
  b you can eat a lot of different types of food
6 a all the accommodation is in hotel suites
  b all the rooms have private bathrooms

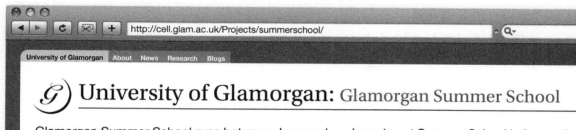

http://cell.glam.ac.uk/Projects/summerschool/

University of Glamorgan   About   News   Research   Blogs

𝒢 University of Glamorgan: Glamorgan Summer School

Glamorgan Summer School runs between June and September. It is an annual event that began over 100 years ago, offering a wide range of taster, day and week-long residential courses.

a *What is the Glamorgan Summer School?*

It is an Adult Education Summer School which gives you the opportunity to learn new skills and to meet people. It's held at the University of Glamorgan, and we're easy to get to by car and public transport. Most of all, it's [1]great value for money, it's friendly – and it's fun!

b _____

Are you over 18? Then you're welcome. We welcome students of all ages and abilities and [2]from all walks of life – qualifications don't matter. We welcome people with learning disabilities, and provide a playscheme and sports camp so [3]parents don't miss out.

c _____

The programme of courses is [4]really varied – Music, Mosaic, Photography, Tai Chi and more!

Learning at Summer School is fun, and you only gain a qualification if that's what you want to do.

d _____

We have lots of free social and cultural entertainment provided by a variety of different groups, with [5]something for every taste. There are discos, concerts, talks and workshops, not forgetting nightly jazz sessions performed by our jazz tutors and their students.

e _____

We are just eight miles from Cardiff, the capital of Wales and a city alive with culture and great nightlife – just a short bus or train ride away. Locally, there are numerous places of historical and cultural interest – and the Brecon Beacons National Park is only a short drive away.

f _____

Students at the Summer School can stay in the excellent [6]en-suite accommodation on the University campus.

1 Before you watch, think about this question: what games or sports did you do when you were young? Do you still do the same things now?

2 Watch the video and match the photos (1–3) with the activities (a–c).

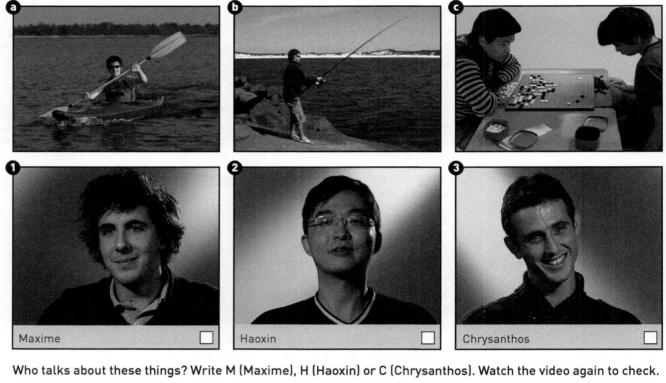

Maxime ☐   Haoxin ☐   Chrysanthos ☐

3 Who talks about these things? Write M (Maxime), H (Haoxin) or C (Chrysanthos). Watch the video again to check.

1 an activity that helps them to meet people: _____ , _____

2 an activity they do in the countryside: _____ , _____

4 Watch Maxime again (00:11–00:56). Number his actions in the right order.

☐ He walked along the beach.   ☐1 He woke up early.
☐ He felt excited.   ☐ He got his fishing stuff.
☐ He waited for the fish to bite.

5 Watch Haoxin again (01:00–01:38). Complete the information about the game that he describes.

The ancient game of *Go* started ¹ _two thousand_ years ago. The rules are simple: the players place ² _____ and ³ _____ stones on a board, which is divided into ⁴ _____ by ⁵ _____ squares. The aim of the game is to control a ⁶ _____ part of the board than the other player.

6 Watch Chrysanthos again (01:42–02:44). Are the sentences true or false?

1 Chrysanthos's brother and sister went rowing at weekends.	TRUE / FALSE
2 Chrysanthos didn't want to go at first.	TRUE / FALSE
3 Chrysanthos didn't like doing any sports.	TRUE / FALSE
4 He didn't like the place or the people where his brother and sister went.	TRUE / FALSE
5 He started kayaking because it was better for his body shape.	TRUE / FALSE

7 Have you tried any of these or any similar activities? Would you like to?

GLOSSARY

stuff (noun): an informal word for *things*
bite (verb): If a fish **bites** when you are fishing, it takes the food or hook in its mouth.
ancient (adjective): very, very old
grid (noun): straight lines that form squares on, for example, paper or a board
board (noun): a square piece of wood or card that you play a game on
rowing /ˈrəʊɪŋ/ (noun): the activity of moving a small kind of boat with no motor ⟶

Work and studies

1 Cross out the word in each group that is *not* correct.

1 I did a course / a subject / a degree in archaeology.
2 I applied to Art College / School / degree.
3 I studied science / maths / exams.
4 I'm writing a thesis / an exam / an essay.
5 I enjoyed the course / a degree / the subject.
6 I passed the college / exam / course.
7 I got a doctorate / an exam / a degree in biology.
8 I went to university / school / studies in the United States.

2 Complete what the people say about their studies with the present perfect of the verbs in brackets. Remember to put the adverbs in the correct position.

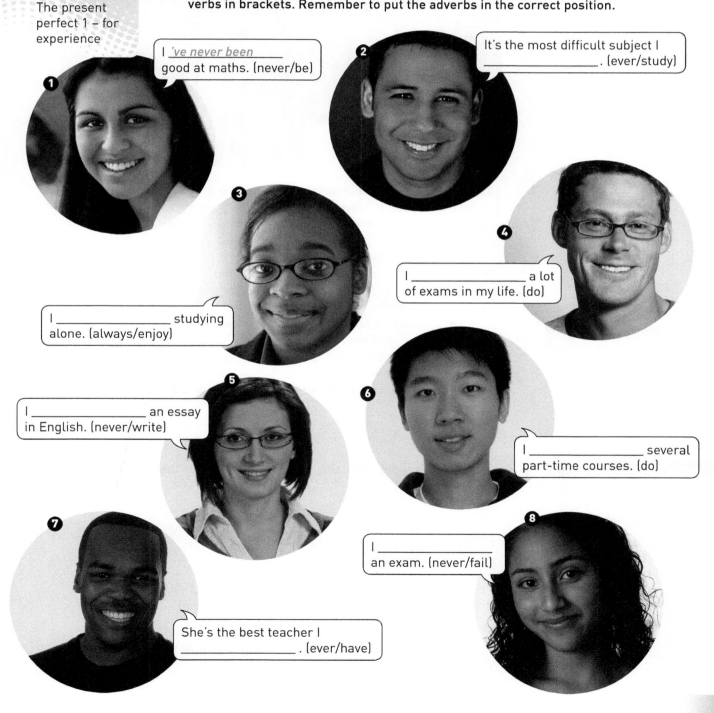

1 I *'ve never been* good at maths. (never/be)

2 It's the most difficult subject I _____. (ever/study)

3 I _____ studying alone. (always/enjoy)

4 I _____ a lot of exams in my life. (do)

5 I _____ an essay in English. (never/write)

6 I _____ several part-time courses. (do)

7 She's the best teacher I _____. (ever/have)

8 I _____ an exam. (never/fail)

3 Complete the magazine article using the words and expressions in the box.

at home   atmosphere   ~~benefits~~   easy   flexible   holiday
management   part-time   pay   place   stressful

Working life
Today, Naseema Bradley talks about her work

I studied accountancy at university, then went to work in the health service as an administration officer. The ¹_____benefits_____ were good – we had five weeks' ²_____ and a private pension plan – but I wasn't happy in my job. The ³_____ wasn't great – I never had any money at the end of the month! – and the work was very ⁴_____ .

Then, after 15 years, our department closed, and I lost my job. It seemed like a disaster, but in fact, it saved my life! After two months, I found a job in a small office. It's a much nicer ⁵_____ to work. We have ⁶_____ working hours, and there's a nice ⁷_____ in the office. The ⁸_____ and my colleagues are very ⁹_____ to work with. And the best thing about it is that it's ¹⁰_____ – three days a week. So I can also do some work ¹¹_____ – I advise people about tax and do their accounts. I work hard, but I organise my own life now and I'm much happier.

4 Complete the sentences using the verbs in the box in the present perfect and *for* or *since*.

be   be   ~~have~~   know   like   live   play   work

1   They _have had_ the same car _for_ ten years.
2   I _____ my boyfriend _____ the 1990s.
3   He _____ a teacher _____ more than 30 years.
4   She _____ for this company _____ a month.
5   We _____ in this flat _____ last April.
6   I _____ science _____ I studied it at primary school.
7   She _____ the guitar _____ she was 12.
8   He _____ with the same company _____ nearly 12 years.

5 Complete this extract from an application letter with the correct prepositions. Be careful – one expression does not need a preposition!

and I am now **looking** [1] _for_ **work** in Human Resources.

As you can see from my CV, I **have a degree** [2]_____ **business studies** and **a diploma** [3]_____ **marketing**. I **have experience** [4]_____ **marketing** and **have been** [5]_____ **PR** for about two years now.

I **enjoy** [6]_____ **working** in a team and **am good** [7]_____ **working** under pressure. I have always **wanted** [8]_____ **work** for a large company and

MYEnglish

6 Read what these people say about using English at work. Are these sentences true or false?

1 Lyudmila doesn't speak English very often. TRUE / FALSE
2 Kamal has difficulty using technical English. TRUE / FALSE
3 Marisa only speaks English when she goes to England. TRUE / FALSE

I make phone calls in English to my colleagues abroad nearly every day.

Lyudmila, Ukraine

Kamal, Sudan

I only use technical language for my work, so I have difficulty with everyday conversation in English, for example when we go out for dinner with clients.

I use English to communicate with our customers in Japan and China.

Marisa, Portugal

Your English

7 Do you use English like these people? Complete the language profile for you.

How do you use English in your job? If you're not working, how would you like to use English in the future? Tick (✓) one or more, or write your answer.	Where have you studied English?	What would be useful for you to improve your English?
Making phone calls ☐	At school or university ☐	Regular English lessons (e.g. one or two a week) ☐
Speaking to people face to face ☐	I've done courses at a language school. ☐	Short courses on specific skills (e.g. telephone English, writing emails) ☐
Reading and writing emails and letters ☐	I've had in-company English training. ☐	An intensive (full immersion) course for a week ☐
Writing reports and presentations ☐	I've done a course in an English-speaking country. ☐	Other _____
Other _____	Other _____	
I never use English at work. ☐	I've never studied English properly. ☐	

If possible, show your profile to your teacher, and ask for their suggestions to improve your English skills.

EXPLOREWriting

8 Read this announcement from a company magazine. Are the sentences true or false?

1 Anyone who works for the company can apply for this opportunity. TRUE / FALSE
2 The company will only pay for the English lessons. TRUE / FALSE

WIN a two-week English course!

Applications in English by email to Simone Lidowski, HR Department, manager.hr@uniton.com

Uniton is offering FIVE of its employees the chance to attend a two-week English course in the UK or United States, with all expenses, including flights and accommodation, paid.

9 Read the email of application. The <u>underlined</u> phrases are inappropriate or too informal. Replace them with phrases from the box.

> advertised
> ~~Dear Ms Lidowski~~
> I enjoy
> I have difficulty in
> I have studied
> I have worked
> I would like
> improve my spoken English
> project the company's image effectively
> Regards

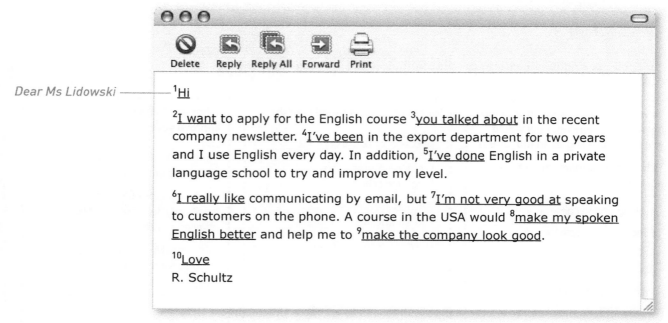

Dear Ms Lidowski ⎯⎯⎯ ¹<u>Hi</u>

²<u>I want</u> to apply for the English course ³<u>you talked about</u> in the recent company newsletter. ⁴<u>I've been</u> in the export department for two years and I use English every day. In addition, ⁵<u>I've done</u> English in a private language school to try and improve my level.

⁶<u>I really like</u> communicating by email, but ⁷<u>I'm not very good at</u> speaking to customers on the phone. A course in the USA would ⁸<u>make my spoken English better</u> and help me to ⁹<u>make the company look good</u>.

¹⁰<u>Love</u>
R. Schultz

10 Write your application for the opportunity in Exercise 8. Include information from your language profile (Exercise 7) and use a polite, formal style.

1 Before you watch, think about this question: have you ever gone to classes to learn something in your free time? What kind of things did you learn?

2 Watch the video and (circle) the correct way to complete the sentences.

Mainda   Paivi

   1 Mainda went to acting classes to …
     a) start a new career.
     b) improve her confidence.
     c) meet people.
   2 Paivi went to dance classes to …
     a) meet people.
     b) become a dance teacher.
     c) learn more about salsa.

3 Watch Mainda again (00:13–00:55) and match the beginnings and endings of the phrases.

1	I took some introductory	a)	voice exercises.
2	The acting classes concentrated on	b)	mooing like cows.
3	There were a lot of	c)	type of acting classes.
4	We did things like	d)	was about.
5	That's what the training	e)	voice projection.

4 Are the sentences about Paivi's classes true or false? Watch again (01:01–02:06) to check.

1	Paivi went to the classes before and after her trip to Cuba.	TRUE / FALSE
2	There was space for about 30 people in the classes.	TRUE / FALSE
3	They had to go with a partner.	TRUE / FALSE
4	They learned about South American and Cuban dance music.	TRUE / FALSE
5	There was a friendly atmosphere in the classes.	TRUE / FALSE

5 Paivi uses the same word in both phrases in each pair. Can you guess what the words are? Watch again to check.

   1 you could fit about 20 _people_ there

       you met lots of _people_ , both women and men

   2 when we came _____ from Cuba

       I went _____ to the classes

   3 I _____ wanted to continue

       it was a _____ great place

   4 we just learned _____ _____ dancing

       I learned _____ _____ about music

   5 the _____ who you meet

       you get _____ from all walks of life

6 Which of these classes would you prefer to go to? Why?

GLOSSARY

moo (verb): make a sound like a cow
role-playing (noun): an activity where you 'act' a situation
got the salsa bug: If you **get the bug** for something, you become very enthusiastic about it.
fit (verb): If you can **fit** something in a place, there is enough space for it.
from all walks of life: people of many different types

How's your food?

1 Look at the word snake and find five more adjectives to describe shops.

endiold-fashionedstendemptylonefriendlyismatconvenientortheexpensivepeatnoisyarnted

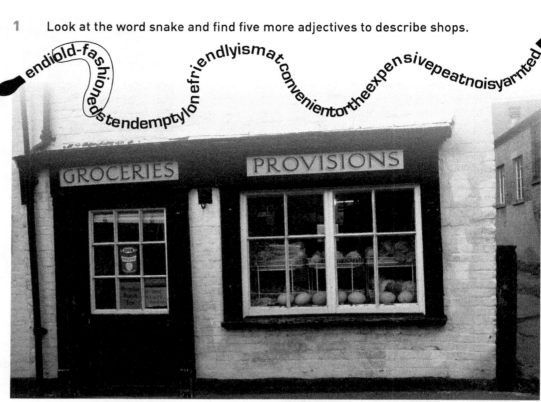

2 Add the vowels to these adjectives. Then match them with their opposites from Exercise 1.

1 _u_ n f r _i_ _e_ n d l y   _friendly_

2 m _ _ d _ _ r n   _____

3 c h _ _ _ p   _____

4 _ n c _ _ n v _ n _ _ _ n t   _____

5 q _ _ _ _ t   _____

6 c r _ _ w d _ d   _____

3 Use some of the adjectives from Exercises 1 and 2 to complete what Patricia says about shopping.

> The market where I buy my fruit and vegetables is always very busy.
> It's ¹ c _rowded_____ and ² n_____ , but the people are always very
> ³ f_____ , and the food is fresh and ⁴ c_____ . It's also very
> ⁵ c_____ because it's only five minutes from where I live.

Patricia, Spain

Over to you

Write a few sentences about how you like to shop. Use some of the adjectives from Exercises 1 and 2.

VOCABULARY
Ordering a meal

4 Who says it? The waiter (W) or the customer (C)?

1 And for you? ☐ W
2 Anything to drink? ☐
3 Are you ready to order? ☐
4 Can we have the bill, please? ☐
5 Sparkling or still? ☐
6 Could we have a bottle of water, please? ☐
7 Yes. I'll have the soup, please. ☐
8 Me too, please – soup. ☐
9 No problem, come this way, please. ☐
10 No, is there a table for two? ☐
11 Of course, I'll bring it for you. ☐
12 Still, please. And two glasses. ☐

5 Now use the sentences from Exercise 4 to complete the dialogues.

Arriving

WAITER Good evening. Do you have a reservation?

CUSTOMER ¹ _No, is there a table for two?_

WAITER ² _____

Ordering

WAITER ³ _____

CUSTOMER Yes. I'll have the soup, please.

WAITER ⁴ _____

CUSTOMER ⁵ _____

WAITER ⁶ _____

CUSTOMER ⁷ _____

WAITER ⁸ _____

CUSTOMER Still, please. And two glasses.

Paying

CUSTOMER ⁹ _____

WAITER Of course. I'll bring it for you.

GRAMMAR
Nouns with prepositional phrases

6 Make prepositional phrases from the box to complete the sentences. Use each phrase only once.

noun	preposition	phrase
~~table~~	with	the corner
meal	in	~~two~~
chicken	for	garlic sauce
bottle	of	red wine
menu		lots of vegetarian dishes
table		25 people

1 Hello. Could I book a _table for two_ for eight thirty, please?
2 To drink, we'll have a _____, please.
3 Do you want to be next to the window, or would you like the _____?
4 I recommend the _____. It's very tasty!
5 I'm cooking a _____ on Saturday – my whole family!
6 There's a good _____ for people who don't eat meat.

7 **Cross out the expression that is *not* possible.**

1   How about / What about / ~~Why don't we~~ some pasta?
2   Perhaps we should / Why don't we / What about get some ice cream?
3   We can / We could / How about put some sausages on the barbecue.
4   What about / What should / What can we make for dessert?
5   Why don't we / How about / We can make a salad for the vegetarians.
6   How about / What should / What about burgers?

Time**Out**

8 **Read the sentences and circle the numbers that are true for you. 1 = Disagree strongly; 5 = Agree strongly**

1   I find supermarkets quite stressful.   1 2 3 4 5
2   Small shops are better, even if things cost more.   1 2 3 4 5
3   Shopping in supermarkets is bad for the environment.   1 2 3 4 5
4   I think supermarkets are crowded and noisy.   1 2 3 4 5
5   Supermarkets are only interested in making money.   1 2 3 4 5

Now add up your total score.

5–11   You like to shop in a place that's cheap and convenient. Why shop in small shops when you can find everything you want in one place?

12–18   You think that supermarkets are unfriendly and bad for the environment, but they make shopping so easy.

19–25   Small shops give you everything you want – great food and friendly service. You hardly ever go to a supermarket.

9 **Complete the crossword.**

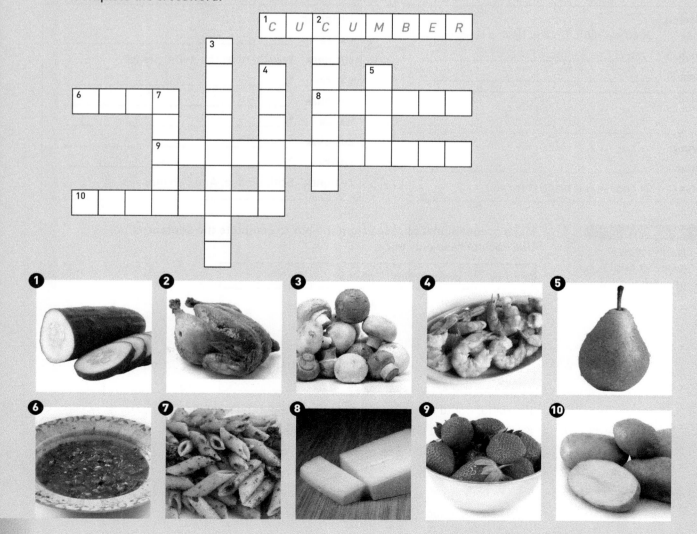

EXPLORE**Reading**

10 Match the sentences (1–4) with the correct heading (a–d).

   a Cost   b Food   c Service   d Setting

  1 The steak was perfect, but the rice was a bit undercooked.
  2 The staff are young, but very good – they did a great job.
  3 The total price was $190 for three of us, which is quite expensive.
  4 It's dark and quiet – the perfect place for a romantic meal for two.

11 Read the reviews. Match the restaurants (1–4) with the food (a–d).

   a chicken curry   c paella
   b lasagne and green salad   d Middle Eastern food

◀ ▶ C + www.mealsout.co.nz	◦Q▾

Reviews   **Add a review**

1 El Buho Azul Murray Street   *Review by: mayfly*

I love El Buho Azul. The food is fantastic, the service is very fast, and the staff are lovely. It's not the most beautiful place in the world, but I don't go to restaurants to look around – I go to eat! And El Buho Azul has the best paella in Wellington. The menu is all Spanish. It's not very good for vegetarians, as most dishes are meat or seafood.

2 Bella Napoli William Street   *Review by: Jorge*

A high-class restaurant with truly excellent food – but don't come here if you like to eat a lot but not pay a lot. It's *very* expensive. The menu is modern Italian – pizzas, pastas and some interesting salads – and the service was very good. All in all, this is the perfect restaurant when you want to go somewhere special and spend a little bit extra.

3 Cedar Tree Parker Avenue   *Review by: PeeCee*

I love Lebanese food, but I was a bit disappointed with the Cedar Tree. The food was not the problem – it was all very good (but the portions were a bit small – I was still hungry after my meal). The big problem was that everything was very slow – we waited more than 45 minutes for our main course. The Cedar Tree is the best place in town for Lebanese food – but don't go there if you want a quick meal!

4 The Taj Percival Street   *Review by: Stroller*

We go to The Taj about once a week. It's cheap, we love the food, and – best of all – the staff love children. My kids are seven and four and they love it when we go to The Taj. The menu has a really wide range of Indian dishes that are very tasty – and very cheap. It's sometimes very noisy – especially when my children are there!

12 Look at what these people say and decide which restaurant is best for them.

> It's my dad's birthday, and I want to take him somewhere special. Money is not a problem! — Pete

> I want to go out for a family meal, but I don't want to spend a lot of money. My husband is vegetarian, but our daughter and I eat meat. — Sonia

> I want somewhere I can have a quick meal before going to the cinema. I don't want somewhere too high class – just quick and tasty. And I want somewhere with good seafood – I don't eat meat. — Ravi

Over to you

Write a website review for a restaurant you know.

1 Before you watch, thin about this question: what do you like to cook? How do you make your favourite food?

2 Look at this list of ingredients. Watch the video and tick (✓) the ones that Nilgun and Alex mention.

almonds	✓	ginger	☐
anchovies	☐	monkey nuts	☐
beef	☐	onions	☐
chicken	☐	pistachios	☐
chilli	☐	potatoes	☐
coconut rice	☐	salmon	☐
garlic	☐	spring onions	☐

3 Nilgun talks about *lokum*, and Alex talks about *nasi lemak*. Which food is each sentence about? Write L (*lokum*) or N (*nasi lemak*).

Nilgun

lokum

Alex

nasi lemak

1 It's sweet. _____

2 It's made with rice. _____

3 It tastes better than it sounds. _____

4 Some kinds are made with nuts. _____

4 Look at what Nilgun says about Haci Bekir, the inventor of *lokum*, and circle the correct answers. Watch again (00:11–01:00) to check.

He ¹has / had a factory in Istanbul many many years ago and he ²becomes / became so famous and he ³opens / opened all these little shops.

5 Look at what Alex says about why he likes cooking and circle the correct answers. Watch again (01:05–02:13) to check.

Cooking ¹is / was a way for me to de-stress myself, so after a long day at work, I ²come / came back and then I ³cook / cooked.

6 What tense does Nilgun mostly use? What tense does Alex mostly use? Why?

7 What is a typical dish from your country? What is it made from? How do you make it?

GLOSSARY

factory (noun): a place where things are made
de-stress (verb): If you **de-stress** yourself, you relax and get away from all the stressful things in your life.
anchovy (noun): a small, very salty fish
pistachios / almonds / monkey nuts (nouns): different kinds of nut

4 Encounters

VOCABULARY
Taxis

1 Complete this section from a guide to Milan, Italy, using the words in the box.

change   fare   meter   passengers   receipt   ~~taxi rank~~   tip

GETTING AROUND
Taxis

In Milan, you can phone for a taxi or get one at a ¹ _taxi rank_ .
Most of them are normal cars and can take four ² _____ , but
there are bigger taxis for more people or disabled passengers. All
drivers use a ³ _____ , and you pay the exact ⁴ _____ at
the end of your journey. The driver will always give you the correct
⁵ _____ , and people don't usually give a ⁶ _____ . If
you need a ⁷ _____ , just ask the driver before you pay.

Milan

Over to you

Write some
information about
taxis for visitors to
your town.

VOCABULARY
Getting a taxi

2 For each of these sentences, decide who's speaking – the taxi driver (T) or
the passenger (P).

1   Just make it 30 dollars.   [P]
2   Have a good trip, then.   []
3   Can you take me to Terminal 2, please?   []
4   So, is this your first time in Sydney?   []
5   Can I have a receipt, please?   []
6   How much is it to the airport?   []
7   That's $27.80, please.   []
8   Can I put my bags in the back?   []

3 Complete the conversation using six of the sentences in Exercise 2.

PASSENGER   Hello. ¹ _____

TAXI DRIVER   Well, it depends on the traffic, but it's usually about 25 to 30 dollars.

PASSENGER   OK, that's fine. ² _____

TAXI DRIVER   I'll do it for you.

PASSENGER   Thanks. ³ _____

***

TAXI DRIVER   Here we are. Terminal 2. ⁴ _____

PASSENGER   Sorry, I've only got $100. And ⁵ _____

TAXI DRIVER   Sure. ⁶ _____

PASSENGER   Thanks. Bye.

4

VOCABULARY

Linking a story

4 Complete this New York taxi story using the time expressions in the box.

> After   During   ~~later~~   then   When

Marina from New York writes:

A cab driver made my wedding day last summer very special.

I was waiting for the limousine to come to my apartment at 11.00. Half an hour ¹ *later* , there was no car and I was getting worried, so I went down to wait in the street. ² _____ a few minutes, a taxi driver stopped and asked if he could help. He helped me get into the taxi with my long white dress, ³ _____ put on a tie to look more professional. ⁴ _____ the journey to the church, he told me I was the first bride he had taken to her wedding in 30 years of driving a taxi! ⁵ _____ we arrived at the church, everyone was very surprised to see me get out of a yellow cab. A truly authentic New York experience.

GRAMMAR

The past progressive

5 Read this email to a taxi firm, and circle the correct verb forms.

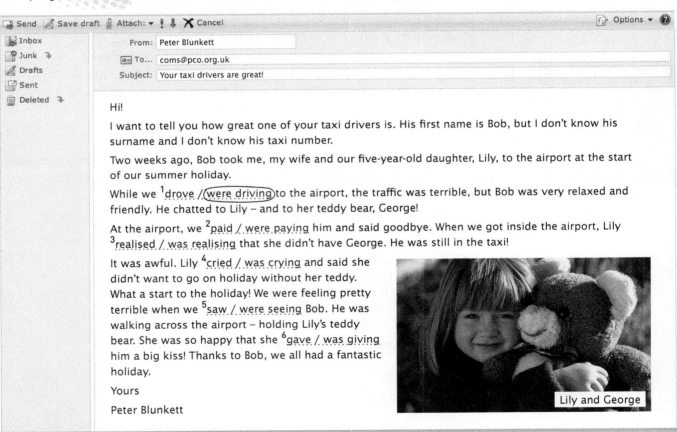

Send   Save draft   Attach: Cancel   Options

Inbox · Junk · Drafts · Sent · Deleted

From: Peter Blunkett
To... coms@pco.org.uk
Subject: Your taxi drivers are great!

Hi!

I want to tell you how great one of your taxi drivers is. His first name is Bob, but I don't know his surname and I don't know his taxi number.

Two weeks ago, Bob took me, my wife and our five-year-old daughter, Lily, to the airport at the start of our summer holiday.

While we ¹drove / were driving to the airport, the traffic was terrible, but Bob was very relaxed and friendly. He chatted to Lily – and to her teddy bear, George!

At the airport, we ²paid / were paying him and said goodbye. When we got inside the airport, Lily ³realised / was realising that she didn't have George. He was still in the taxi!

It was awful. Lily ⁴cried / was crying and said she didn't want to go on holiday without her teddy. What a start to the holiday! We were feeling pretty terrible when we ⁵saw / were seeing Bob. He was walking across the airport – holding Lily's teddy bear. She was so happy that she ⁶gave / was giving him a big kiss! Thanks to Bob, we all had a fantastic holiday.

Yours

Peter Blunkett

Lily and George

VOCABULARY

Starting a story

6 Complete the sentences for starting a story using *for, in, to, with* or – (no preposition).

1   I was living __*in*__ Caracas.
2   I was going _____ Mexico.
3   I was working _____ a bar.
4   I was travelling _____ Europe.
5   I was visiting _____ Hong Kong.

6   I was waiting _____ my flight.
7   I was _____ some friends.
8   I was looking _____ a hostel.
9   I was on my way _____ the airport.
10   It was _____ winter, and very cold.

MYEnglish

7 Read what these people say in the *Cambridge Encyclopedia of Language*. Match them with their reasons for learning English (a–e).

> When I finish learning English, my pay as secretary will increase by nearly ten times.

1 trainee secretary, Egypt

> My company plans big deals with the Arabic world. None of us speak Arabic, and they do not know Japanese. All our plans and meetings are in English.

2 businessman, Japan

> Nearly everyone in Denmark speaks English. If we didn't, there wouldn't be anyone to talk to.

> After I learned English, I felt I was in touch with the international world for the very first time.

4 doctor, India

> If I want to keep up to date with the latest techniques and products, I must certainly maintain my English very strongly.

5 university student, Denmark

3 teacher, Nigeria

I need English ...
a ... to feel I am part of the global community. ☐ 3
b ... to learn about new things in my job. ☐
c ... for communicating in my work. ☐
d ... because my language is not spoken outside my country. ☐
e ... to have more money. ☐

8 Look at sentences a–e in Exercise 7 and match the sentence halves to complete the rules.

1 We use **to** ...
2 We use **for** ...
3 We use **because** ...

a ... to join two sentences.
b ... before an infinitive verb.
c ... before an –ing verb.

9 Complete these other reasons for learning English with *to*, *for* or *because*.

I learn English ...

1 __to__ read books or magazines about things I'm interested in.
2 _____ I like watching films in the original language.
3 _____ improve my chances of getting a good job.
4 _____ chatting with people on the Internet.
5 _____ a lot of my favourite musicians sing in English.
6 _____ I attend international meetings and conferences.
7 _____ writing emails to colleagues and clients.
8 _____ communicate with people when I travel.

Your English

10 Why are you learning English? Tick the reasons in Exercises 7 and 9 that are true for you, and add any other reasons.

EXPLORE Writing

11 Read this email to a taxi firm and choose the correct reason why Rosa is writing.

a to complain about something
b to ask for help

File Edit View Insert Format Tools Message Help

To: Info@eurocabs.org
From: Rosa Dalecka
Date: 29 September
Subject: Lost bag

1 Yesterday evening, I travelled in one of your taxis, and at the end of my journey, I left a bag in the back of the car.

2 I was travelling from the train station to my home in Woodfield Road at about 7 p.m. Unfortunately, I do not know the number of the taxi, but I think it was a VW, and the driver was a woman.

3 The bag is a small, grey backpack with orange zips and straps. It contained some books, an umbrella and some photocopies and notes.

4 Could you please tell me if you have found this bag and if so, where I can get it back?

Many thanks.
Rosa Dalecka

12 Which paragraph of the email ...

a asks for information? ☐
b gives details of the bag? ☐
c describes the problem? ☐
d gives details of the taxi journey? ☐

13 Choose words from the table or add other words to describe a bag you use.

It's a	small	black	plastic	backpack	with	wheels.
	medium	red	leather	shopping bag		straps.
	big	brown	cotton	bag		a zip.

14 Imagine you left your bag in a taxi. Write an email to the taxi company. Don't forget to:

- say when and where you were travelling
- describe the bag and what is in it
- ask where you can get it back.

1 Before you watch, try to complete this table.

Country	Nationality	Main languages
¹ _Switzerland_	Swiss	German, ² _____ and Italian
Japan	³ _____	⁴ _____
⁵ _____	Afghan	Pashto and Dari
⁶ _____	Indian	Hindi and English

2 The missing words from Exercise 1 are all in the video. What do you think Lona talks about? Watch the video and check your answers in the table.

Lona

3 Watch the video again. Use words from the table in Exercise 1 to complete these sentences about Lona's encounter.

1 Lona was in _____ at the time.
2 The man she met was _____ . His wife was _____ .
3 The man was wearing traditional _____ clothes.
4 Lona and the man spoke in _____ first, then in _____ .
5 The man's wife also spoke _____ and _____ as second languages.
6 The man had travelled in _____ and _____ .
7 Lona and the man also chatted in _____ .

4 Lona uses a lot of adjectives to describe her experience. Use the adjectives in the box to complete these phrases from the video. Watch again to check.

> beautiful   beautiful   little   ~~magnificent~~   nice   unusual

1 There's a _magnificent_ lake, which is very _____ .
2 There was one family that looked very _____ .
3 He was wearing something that seemed quite _____ .
4 They had two _____ kids.
5 That was a very _____ experience.

5 Watch again and ⟨circle⟩ the words that Lona uses to say why this was an interesting encounter.

It was just like a complete ¹⟨mix⟩/ mixture of culture, and for me that ²man / family demonstrated an acceptance of ³different / several cultures and they had ⁴really / actually incorporated different cultures into their ⁵lives / lifestyle.

6 Have you ever had a similar multicultural or multilingual encounter?

GLOSSARY

loose-fitting (adjective): **Loose-fitting** clothes are comfortable and not tight.
robe (noun): a type of long dress worn by both men and women
pointy (adjective): **Pointy** shoes have a point at the toes.
turban (noun): a long piece of cloth which is worn wrapped around the head
acceptance (noun): If you **accept** something (or show **an acceptance** of something), it has become normal for you.
incorporated into: included, or made a part of something

5 Money

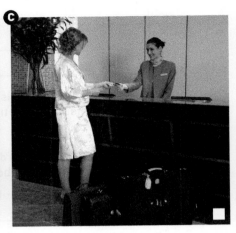

VOCABULARY

Money

1 Look at the conversations in Exercises 2–4 and write the correct numbers on the photos.

2 Number the conversation in the correct order.

___ Sorry, do you have any smaller notes?
_1_ Hello. Can I change these euros into Canadian dollars, please?
___ Sure. Are twenties OK?
___ Of course. That's 50, 100, 150, 200 euros. So that's $332.22. Here you are.
___ Fine. Thanks.

3 Complete the conversation using the words in the box.

~~bill~~ cards pay PIN receipt

A Could I have the ¹_____bill_____, please? Room 13.

B Certainly. How would you like to ²_____?

A Do you take ³_____?

B Yes, we do. Just a moment. Can you type in your ⁴_____, please?

A Sure.

B That's fine, and here's your ⁵_____.

4 Put the words in the correct order to complete the conversation.

A OK. That's one day return ticket to Cardiff. ¹to / you / How / like / pay / would / ?
B Sorry, ²is / how / much / it / ?
A £13.80.
B OK, ³cash / in / pay / I'll / .
A ⁴have / you / smaller / Do / anything / ?
B Sorry, no. That's all I've got.

GRAMMAR

have to, can

5 Match 1–5 with a–e.

1 Can I get a student ticket?   a No, sorry. You have to pay in cash.
2 Do I have to book my ticket in   b Yes, but you have to show your
  advance?   student card.
3 Can I pay by card?   c Oh, OK. Can I pay by card?
4 I have to change some dollars.   d No, you don't have to do that, but
5 Sorry, we can't accept euros.   it's a good idea.
                                   e You can do that in the hotel.

VOCABULARY
Giving advice

6 (Circle) the correct expressions to complete the advice and rules for visitors to these places.

1 You don't have to / (can't) take photos.
2 You can / shouldn't smoke here.
3 You don't have to / can't pay if you live here.
4 You should / don't have to switch off your mobile.
5 Don't / You don't have to drive your car here.
6 You don't have to / shouldn't wear shoes.
7 You can / shouldn't take glasses out of the pub.
8 You don't have to / should put your books back.
9 You shouldn't / have to leave things in your room.
10 Don't / You have to show your ticket here.

TimeOut

7 Complete the crossword with money words.

ACROSS

2 You have to pay your electricity, gas and water ____bills____.
4 This is the official money in a country, e.g. euros or dollars.
5 You can get money from a bank or a _____ machine.
6 This type of money is made of metal.
7 If you use your card to pay, you usually need this number.
8 The euro has _____ of 500, 200, 100, 50, 20, 10 and 5.

DOWN

1 This is the money used in the USA, Canada, Australia and other countries.
2 You can pay for things in cash or _____ card.
3 When you buy something, you usually get a _____.
4 When you arrive in a country, you can _____ money at the airport.

EXPLORE**Reading**

8 Look at the travel web page opposite giving advice for people going to India. Tick (✓) the money services that are mentioned.

1 banks ☑
2 cash machines ☐
3 traveller's cheques ☐
4 credit cards ☐
5 private money changers ☐
6 airport exchange banks ☐
7 international money transfers ☐
8 cash advances (getting cash with your credit card) ☐
9 hotel exchange desks ☐

9 Read the information on the web page and decide if these tips are good or bad advice.

Money tips – India

1 It's a good idea to always have some cash with you.   GOOD / BAD

2 Leave your passport in the hotel; you don't need it to change money.   GOOD / BAD

3 Take your card – you'll find an ATM in every town and village.   GOOD / BAD

4 Don't keep the emergency lost-and-stolen phone numbers with your credit card.   GOOD / BAD

5 Take US or Australian dollars; you can change these everywhere.   GOOD / BAD

6 Remember to change your rupees before you leave India.   GOOD / BAD

7 Don't go to private money changers.   GOOD / BAD

8 You should take traveller's cheques in pounds sterling or US dollars.   GOOD / BAD

10 Look at the <u>underlined</u> words on the web page. They can have more than one meaning. Which meaning is correct here?

1 denominations
   a the values or units of coins or banknotes
   b different types of Christianity
2 backup
   a a copy of data on a computer
   b something extra which you can use if you need
3 maintain
   a always have with you
   b repair regularly to keep in good condition
4 leftover
   a not used
   b not eaten
5 wire
   a connect a piece of electrical equipment
   b send money electronically
6 proof-of-purchase slip
   a a receipt from a shop to show you have bought something
   b a receipt from a bank to show you have changed money

Over to you

Write some money tips for people visiting your country.

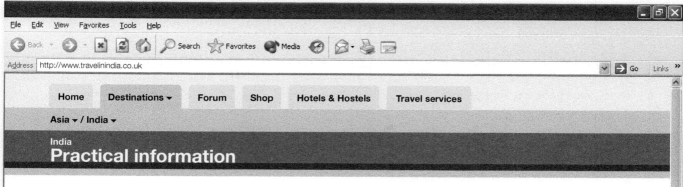

File Edit View Favorites Tools Help

Back | Search | Favorites | Media

Address http://www.travelinindia.co.uk | Go | Links »

| Home | Destinations ▼ | Forum | Shop | Hotels & Hostels | Travel services |

Asia ▼ / India ▼

India
Practical information

INDIA
Overview
Places in India
When to go & weather
Getting there & around
Practical information
  Money & costs
  Health & safety
  Visas
Work & study

Money

The Indian rupee (Rs) is divided into 100 paise (p). Coins come in <u>denominations</u> of 5, 10, 20, 25 and 50 paise, and Rs 1, 2 and 5; notes come in Rs 10, 20, 50, 100, 500 and 1,000. The Indian rupee is linked to a number of currencies, and its value is generally stable.

Remember, you must present your passport whenever you change currency or traveller's cheques.

ATMs

Modern 24-hour ATMs (cash machines) are found in most large towns and cities. Away from major towns, always carry cash or traveller's cheques as <u>backup</u>.

Always keep the emergency lost-and-stolen numbers for your credit cards in a safe place, separate from your cards, and report any loss or theft immediately.

Cash

Major currencies, such as US dollars, UK pounds and euros, are easy to change throughout India. A few banks also accept Australian, New Zealand and Canadian dollars, and Swiss francs. Private money changers accept a wider range of currencies.

Nobody in India ever seems to have change, so it's a good idea to <u>maintain</u> a stock of smaller currency: Rs 10, 20 and 50 notes.

You cannot take rupees out of India. However, you can change any <u>leftover</u> rupees back into foreign currency, most easily at the airport. Note that some airport banks will only change a minimum of Rs 1,000. You may require encashment certificates or a credit-card receipt, and you may also have to show your passport and airline ticket.

Credit cards

Credit cards are accepted at many shops, restaurants and hotels, and you can also use them to pay for flights and train tickets. Cash advances on major credit cards are also possible at some banks without ATMs. MasterCard and Visa are the most widely accepted cards.

International transfers

If you run out of money, someone at home can <u>wire</u> you money via money changers affiliated with Moneygram or Western Union.

Money changers

Private money changers are usually open for longer hours than banks, and they are found almost everywhere (many also double as internet cafés and travel agents). Some upmarket hotels may also change money, usually at well below the bank rate.

Traveller's cheques

All major brands are accepted in India, but some banks may only accept cheques from Amex and Thomas Cook. Pounds sterling and US dollars are the safest currencies, especially in smaller towns.

If you lose your cheques, contact the Amex or Thomas Cook office in Delhi. To replace lost traveller's cheques, you need the <u>proof-of-purchase slip</u> and the numbers of the missing cheques (some places require a photocopy of the police report and a passport photo).

1 Before you watch, think about this question: how do you manage your money? Tick (✓) the things you do.

1 carry cash with you   ☐ _AL_
2 use a credit card   ☐ _____
3 use internet banking   ☐ _____
4 check your bank account online   ☐ _____
5 go into a branch of your bank   ☐ _____
6 send money by mobile phone   ☐ _____
7 ring your bank to check your account   ☐ _____
8 go into a shop to send money to someone   ☐ _____

2 Watch the video. Who talks about doing the things in Exercise 1? Write AL (Anna Laura) or M (Mainda).

Anna Laura

Mainda

3 Are the sentences true or false? Watch the video again to help you.

1 Anna Laura thinks cash is better than credit cards when travelling.   TRUE / FALSE
2 Anna Laura thinks it's easier to check her account online than to go to a bank.   TRUE / FALSE
3 Anna Laura's father has started to use online banking.   TRUE / FALSE
4 Mainda says there have been big changes in mobile phone technology in recent years.   TRUE / FALSE
5 Mainda thinks sending money by mobile is not a good use of technology.   TRUE / FALSE

4 Anna Laura talks about her father's problems with online banking. Circle the correct verb forms to complete the extract, then watch again (00:11–01:13) to check.

My father, who is 82, ¹has recently discovered / is recently discovering how wonderful it is to use internet banking, but the problem with him, because he's 82, ²he's only learning / he's only learned very recently how to use a computer, and so when ³he's done / he's doing his internet banking things, ⁴he gets / he's getting stuck and ⁵picks up / picked up the phone to me.

5 Which is the correct description of how to send money by phone, according to Mainda?

1 You pay money in a shop and send a text message to another person. That person uses the message to collect the money from another shop.
2 You pay money in a shop. The shop sends the money to another shop, which sends a text message to the other person to collect the money.

6 Have you ever sent money to someone in another town or country? How did you do it?

GLOSSARY

wherever you are, wherever I am: in any place or situation
branch (noun): one of the offices of a bank or company
state (noun): the condition or situation of something at the moment
get stuck (verb): If you **get stuck** when you are doing something, you can't go on because it's difficult or you have a problem.
for instance: for example
user (noun): a person who uses a service or a product

Energy

VOCABULARY
Household chores

1 Complete the advice on this website about household chores.

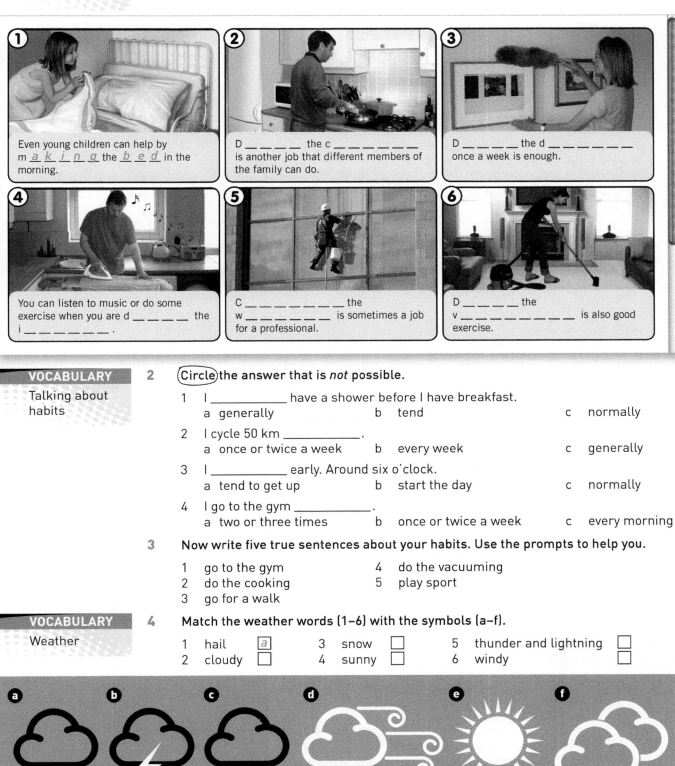

① Even young children can help by m _a k i n g_ the _b e d_ in the morning.

② D _ _ _ _ _ _ the c _ _ _ _ _ _ _ _ is another job that different members of the family can do.

③ D _ _ _ _ _ _ the d _ _ _ _ _ _ _ once a week is enough.

④ You can listen to music or do some exercise when you are d _ _ _ _ _ _ the i _ _ _ _ _ _ _ .

⑤ C _ _ _ _ _ _ _ _ _ the w _ _ _ _ _ _ _ _ is sometimes a job for a professional.

⑥ D _ _ _ _ _ _ the v _ _ _ _ _ _ _ _ _ is also good exercise.

VOCABULARY
Talking about habits

2 ⟨Circle⟩ the answer that is *not* possible.

1 I _____ have a shower before I have breakfast.
   a generally   b tend   c normally

2 I cycle 50 km _____ .
   a once or twice a week   b every week   c generally

3 I _____ early. Around six o'clock.
   a tend to get up   b start the day   c normally

4 I go to the gym _____ .
   a two or three times   b once or twice a week   c every morning

3 Now write five true sentences about your habits. Use the prompts to help you.

1 go to the gym   4 do the vacuuming
2 do the cooking   5 play sport
3 go for a walk

VOCABULARY
Weather

4 Match the weather words (1–6) with the symbols (a–f).

1 hail   a   3 snow ☐   5 thunder and lightning ☐
2 cloudy ☐   4 sunny ☐   6 windy ☐

5 **Match the different kinds of weather in the box to the explanations (1–6).**

A rainbow   Hail   Heavy rain   Lightning   ~~Thunder~~   Tornado

---

www.wheredoesweathercomefrom.com

1 *Thunder*

The lightning makes the air around it very, very hot – up to 33,000°C. As this air gets cooler, it makes a shock wave, and this is the loud sound that we hear. The closer the lightning is, the louder the noise we hear.

2 _____

Large electrical fields build up in the clouds. When they become very large, they 'spark', and this causes the flash of light that we see, as the electrical energy travels between the clouds and the ground.

3 _____

Sometimes in a thunderstorm, warm, wet air meets hot, dry air, and the wind makes it spin in a circle. The warm, wet air is pulled upwards and makes a giant column of air. They can reach speeds of up to 480kph.

4 _____

Warm air rises and forms drops of water. These drops join together in clouds. When the drops get big enough and get heavier, they fall from the sky.

5 _____

Strong winds lift rain high into the sky where it freezes and becomes ice. The ice is heavy, so it falls to the ground.

6 _____

When sunlight meets water in the air, the light is split into its different colours. The physics is complicated, but from the ground it looks like the light is 'bent' to make an arch.

GRAMMAR

Comparing things

6 **Circle the correct form of the adjectives.**

1   Sydney is the big / bigger / **biggest** city in Australia.
2   In Australia, December is usually hot / hotter / hottest than August.
3   The Sydney Festival is the important / more important / most important arts festival in Australia.
4   Melbourne is far / further / furthest south than Sydney.
5   The Opera House is a beautiful / more beautiful / most beautiful building.
6   Rugby League is the popular / more popular / most popular sport in Sydney.

7 **Complete the paragraph about Hong Kong with the adjectives from the box in the correct form.**

cloudy   cool   ~~good~~   hot   wet

Over to you

Write some sentences about the weather in your country.
What is the hottest time of year?
When is the best time of year to visit?
When is it wettest?

The ¹_____*best*_____ months to visit Hong Kong are November and December. The temperature then is ²_____ than it is in summer, and it is usually dry, too. January and February are also cool, but you might not see so much sun because it is ³_____ than November and December.
May to August is the ⁴_____ part of the year, with temperatures of over 30°C. August is also the ⁵_____ month of the year, with 390mm of rain, on average.

MYEnglish

8 Sandra is learning English in London. Read her self-assessment form. Which things does Sandra find difficult?

1 Talking about habits   3 Speaking politely
2 Talking about the weather   4 Prepositions

Sandra, Sweden

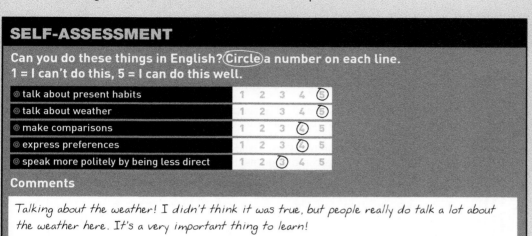

SELF-ASSESSMENT

Can you do these things in English? Circle a number on each line.
1 = I can't do this, 5 = I can do this well.

	1	2	3	4	5
◉ talk about present habits	1	2	3	4	⑤
◉ talk about weather	1	2	3	4	⑤
◉ make comparisons	1	2	3	④	5
◉ express preferences	1	2	3	④	5
◉ speak more politely by being less direct	1	2	③	4	5

Comments

Talking about the weather! I didn't think it was true, but people really do talk a lot about the weather here. It's a very important thing to learn!

I think I can do most of these things well apart from the last one. I think it's difficult to get the right level of politeness in English. Swedish feels much more direct than English. I worry that if I try to translate from Swedish into English, I will be too direct and people might be upset or think that I am rude. People here say 'to be honest' a lot. It makes me think they aren't honest when they don't say it!

(And another thing – it isn't on the form, but I still have a big problem with prepositions! I still translate from Swedish and say 'in' too much. I need to learn my prepositions!)

Your English

9 What about you? Do you think it is difficult to speak more politely in English? Do you think it is *important* to be polite in English?

10 Make these sentences less direct (and therefore more polite). Use some of the expressions from the box to help you.

really   Would you mind -ing?   Do you think you could … ?   Could you … ?   please   not very

1 Wait here.   *Would you mind waiting here? / Could you wait here, please?*

2 I don't like football. _____

3 Be quiet. _____

4 This is boring. _____

5 What time is it? _____

11 Sandra also said she had a problem with prepositions. Are prepositions in your language different from English prepositions?

12 Complete the sentences using the prepositions in the box.

at   for   in   ~~in~~   on

1 What's the weather like __*in*__ your country?

2 Manuel bought a treadmill and put it _____ the corner of his office.

3 He got better _____ working while he walked.

4 Alex cycles _____ 45 minutes to wash and dry his clothes.

5 The fastest winds _____ Earth are inside a tornado.

EXPLOREWriting

13 Read the hotel reviews from a review web page and answer this question: Who liked the Silver Bear Hotel, Peter H or Matt C?

Silver Bear Hotel, Oslo
★★★

Peter H from Lisbon **recommends** *this hotel.*
I was very pleased with this beautiful hotel. The room was big, and the bathroom was great. Also, I think it's the cleanest hotel I have ever stayed in. The staff were friendlier than in other hotels I have visited in Oslo. They were always ready to help.
The hotel is a little far from the city centre, but it's in a quiet area and it was easy to get to the centre by public transport. I'd rather have a comfortable hotel at a good price than be right in the city centre.
Just one complaint – the breakfast could have been better, but apart from that I would definitely recommend this hotel.

Matt C from London **does not recommend** *this hotel.*
A very disappointing stay. The room was big, but the bathroom wasn't very clean, and the towels were too small – the bed was uncomfortable, too.
I prefer to stay near the city centre, and this hotel is too far from there – a long tram ride.
The hotel staff were rude and unhelpful, and as well as that, this has to be the worst place in the city to change money.
I have stayed in Oslo several times, and this is the worst hotel I've stayed in in the city. I won't be going back.

14 Write the adjectives and adjectival phrases in the correct column of the table.

~~big~~   comfortable   could have been better   disappointing   far from the centre   friendly   great   in a quiet area   not very clean   ready to help   rude   too small   uncomfortable   unhelpful

positive	negative
big	

15 Complete the sentences from another hotel review using the expressions in the box.

could have been cleaner   don't mind   more expensive   ~~The best~~   would prefer

1 Very good. _*The best*_ hotel I have ever stayed in.
2 The room was OK, but it _____. The windows in our room were very dirty.
3 I _____ to stay somewhere nearer the centre.
4 The hotel is OK if you _____ the noise of the motorway outside.
5 It is _____ than other hotels in the city.

16 Match the indirect / more polite sentences (1–5) with their more direct meaning (a–e).

1 It could be cheaper.   a It took an hour by bus.
2 It wasn't very close to the city centre.   b It tasted horrible.
3 The bed could have been more comfortable.   c It's very expensive.
4 The food wasn't very good.   d It was impossible to sleep.
5 The room was a bit small.   e It was *very* small!

17 Write a review for the web page of a hotel you have stayed in. It can be a good review or a bad review. If you can't think of a hotel, invent one. Think about: the rooms, the staff, the location.

1   Before you watch, think about this question: what's your favourite season?
What's the weather like at that time of year?

Freda

Anna

Laura

2   Watch the video and match the topics (a–c) with the speakers (1–3).

a   the different climates in one country
b   a very cold holiday
c   the differences between summer and winter

3   Watch again. Are the sentences true or false?

1 People in Finland talk more in winter.	TRUE / FALSE
2 In Finland, people stay at home more in summer.	TRUE / FALSE
3 Anna likes the climate in Australia.	TRUE / FALSE
4 The coldest parts of Australia are in the mountains and in the south.	TRUE / FALSE
5 Laura left Rio de Janeiro in winter.	TRUE / FALSE
6 Laura and her friends had the wrong clothes for Tierra del Fuego.	TRUE / FALSE

4   Watch Freda again (00:11–00:50). Complete the sentences using *quite* or *really*.

1   The summer in Finland is _____ warm, and the days are _____ , _____ long. In the winter, it's cold and
it's dark, and the days are _____ short. And people are _____ different in the summer.

2   In the winter, people tend to be just _____ shy and they don't speak as much to each other.

5   Watch Anna again (00:55–01:46). Circle the correct word to complete these sentences.

1   Anna really / quite likes Australia.
2   The climate is really / quite hot inland, close to the desert.
3   When you get closer to the Antarctic, the climate gets really / quite cold.
4   Anna thinks there's really / quite a lot of choice of different climates in Australia.

6   Watch Laura again (01:51–02:27). Write *really* (x3) and *quite* (x1) in the correct places to complete this
summary of her story.

really
It was ∧ hot when they left Rio de Janeiro, but when
they got to Tierra del Fuego, it was cold. They didn't
have the right clothes, but they wrapped up warm
with all the clothes they had. They stayed indoors a
lot, but they did go out and see some penguins.

7   What's the climate like in your country? Is it very different in different parts of the country?

GLOSSARY

the tropics (plural noun): the band of the earth immediately north and south of the equator
inland (adjective): away from the sea
the height of summer: the middle of summer, the hottest part of summer
resort to (verb): If you **resort to** something, you do something you wouldn't usually do – perhaps because you have no choice.

7 City life

1 Complete what the people say about environmental problems using the words in the box.

> climate   flooding   ~~gas~~   oil   polluted   sea level   traffic   transport

1 It's really important that we use more energy from sun and wind, and less from _____*gas*_____ and _____.

2 We had really heavy rain and a lot of _____ in our area last year.

3 The air here is really _____ ; there are just too many cars.

4 Now petrol is so expensive, maybe there'll be less _____ on the roads.

5 I live on the coast, and the _____ is rising every year.

6 I know _____ change is a serious problem, but for us it's nice to have warmer summers!

7 We need to develop more efficient forms of _____ for the future.

2 Look at the statements in Exercise 1 again.

1 Which person quite likes the result of climate change?
2 Which two people describe problems related to water?
3 Which two people describe changes we need to make?
4 Which person hopes to see a positive result from a problem?

3 Match the sentences (1–3) with the definitions (a–c).

1 The traffic in the city will get worse.
2 There won't be more flooding in the future.
3 The sea might (not) become more polluted.

a I'm sure this will happen.
b It's possible that this will happen.
c There's no chance that this will happen.

4 What do you think city life will be like in 2050? Complete the sentences with *will*, *won't*, *might* or *may* to give your opinion.

1 People _____ leave big cities; they _____ live in smaller towns.
2 City transport _____ be very different from today.
3 Rich people _____ live in the city centres.
4 Buildings _____ become taller.
5 Old historic cities _____ be destroyed to build more efficient towns.
6 It _____ become less expensive to live in a city.
7 Schools and universities _____ be on campuses outside the cities.
8 Green space and parks _____ be used for building houses.
9 It _____ be more difficult to find work in the cities.
10 People _____ stay at home more in their free time.

What other changes do you think there will be in city life in the future? Write a sentence or record yourself speaking on the DVD-ROM.

34

Real conditionals

5 Match the two parts of the sentences.

1 If you leave now,
2 If you like Italian food,
3 If you go there in spring,
4 If you buy a smaller car,
5 If you like world music,
6 If you write to the company,

a you should listen to this band.
b they might send you some information.
c you'll see the trees full of flowers.
d you'll pay less for petrol.
e you should go to Pizza Plus.
f you might get the five o'clock train.

6 Circle the correct verb forms to complete the sentences.

1 Daniel helps / will help her tomorrow if she has / she'll have any problems.
2 If you go / you'll go to the end of the road, you see / you'll see a cinema on your left.
3 I send / I'll send you the photo if I find / I'll find it.
4 If I have / I might have time, I call / I might call them.
5 If you go / you should go to New York, you go / you should go to Central Park.
6 If you look / you'll look on my desk, you see / you'll see a black diary.

Giving directions

7 Look at the map of the city centre and follow the directions a local person gives the tourist at the train station. Find the tourist office on the map: a, b, c or d.

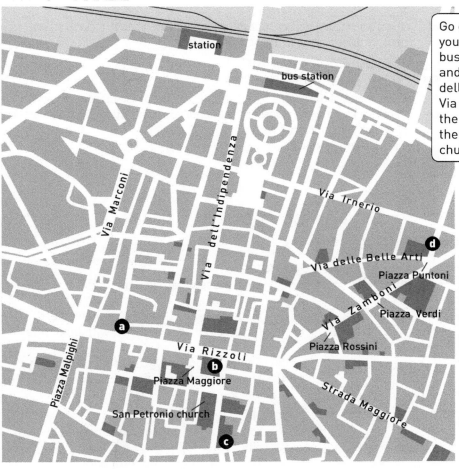

Go out of here and turn left. When you get to the lights, you'll see the bus station in front of you. Turn right and go up the big street called Via dell'Indipendenza. If you continue along Via dell'Indipendenza, you'll come to the main square, Piazza Maggiore. It's there, on your left, opposite the big church of San Petronio.

8 Complete the directions from the tourist office to the art gallery using the phrases in the box.

Go along   go past   on your   ~~out of~~   turn   you continue   you'll come   you'll see

Go ¹ _out of_ here and go back to Via Rizzoli. Turn right and ² _____ two big towers in front of you. ³ _____ Via Rizzoli, and when you come to the towers, ⁴ _____ left down Via Zamboni. If ⁵ _____ down this road, you'll ⁶ _____ two small squares ⁷ _____ right, then ⁸ _____ to another little square, called Piazza Puntoni. The gallery is on the corner of that square, in Via delle Belle Arti.

9 **Cross out the word that does *not* go with each bold phrase.**

1 **I'm looking for** a bed and breakfast / ~~day trips~~ / somewhere to stay.
2 **Do you organise** city tours / trips / a map ?
3 **Have you got** a map / a restaurant / any leaflets ?
4 **Can you recommend** somewhere to eat / a good hotel / leaflets ?
5 **Do you have any information about** the bus station / museums / things to do ?
6 **Do you sell** guidebooks / travel passes / art galleries ?

10 **Complete the tourist's questions in the tourist office. Use the expressions in bold from Exercise 9.**

TOURIST OFFICER	Hello, can I help you?
TOURIST	Yes, I've just arrived, and ¹ *I'm looking for* the bed and breakfast I booked online. ² _____ a map?
TOURIST OFFICER	Yes, here you are. We're here, in the main square.
TOURIST	OK, thanks. And ³ _____ the museums or other things to see?
TOURIST OFFICER	Right, here's a leaflet about all the museums and galleries, but it's a nice city just to walk around.
TOURIST	⁴ _____ any city tours?
TOURIST OFFICER	There's a walking tour in English tomorrow morning at 11 o'clock, starting from here. Or there's a bus tour that goes all day.
TOURIST	⁵ _____ tickets for that?
TOURIST OFFICER	No, you can just pay the bus driver.
TOURIST	Great. One last question – ⁶ _____ a cheap restaurant near here?
TOURIST OFFICER	There's a pizzeria just across the square, or you'll find lots of cafés and fast-food places all along this road here.
TOURIST	OK. Thanks very much.

TimeOut

11 **Complete the crossword. All the answers are places in a city.**

Across clue 3: G A L L E R Y

ACROSS

3 It's a place where you go to see pictures or other works of art.
7 If you travel by train, you'll arrive here.
8 It's an open area in a city, with buildings around it.
9 This is a good way to visit a new place.
10 This is a waterway (in cities like Amsterdam and Venice).

DOWN

1 You can go here to get information about a city. (2 words)
2 This is another word for a park.
4 It's a place where you can see a collection of interesting things.
5 It's a big house where a royal or important family lives.
6 These are the interesting things you can see in a city or country.

EXPLORE Reading

12 Look at the web page about a short holiday in Cork, Ireland. Match the headings (1–9) with the information the sections contain (a–i).

1	Why go now?		a	a trip out of town
2	Touch down		b	a good time to visit
3	Check in		c	museums and galleries
4	Take a hike		d	somewhere to have a drink
5	Cultural afternoon		e	arriving at the airport
6	Window shopping		f	looking around the shops
7	An aperitif		g	somewhere to stay
8	Dining with the locals		h	a sightseeing walk
9	Take a ride		i	dinner in a restaurant

13 Read the information. Are these sentences true or false?

1	It's dark in summer before 9 p.m.	TRUE / FALSE
2	The only transport from the airport is by taxi.	TRUE / FALSE
3	There is only one hostel in Cork.	TRUE / FALSE
4	Grand Parade was a canal before it was a street.	TRUE / FALSE
5	Butter was important in Cork's history.	TRUE / FALSE
6	It's difficult to find traditional Irish pubs.	TRUE / FALSE
7	Blarney Castle is in the centre of Cork.	TRUE / FALSE

Over to you

Do you think you would enjoy 48 hours in Cork? Write two sentences saying what you would do there.

14 According to the article, who would enjoy 48 hours in Cork?

1 people who enjoy walking in the countryside
2 only people who are interested in food and drink
3 people who like sightseeing and culture
4 young people who like clubbing

---

http://www.independenttravel/48-hours-in/cork.html

Home > Travel > 48 Hours In

Cork

▽ SHARE | 🖶 PRINT ARTICLE | ✉ EMAIL ARTICLE | ᴀᴀ TEXT SIZE

by Simon Calder

Click here for 48 hours in ... Cork map

Why go now?
Ireland's second city is an ideal summer destination: friendly, compact, lively – and far enough west for the evening light in August to continue past 9 p.m.

Touch down
Non-stop flights operate to Cork from a wide range of British airports. Cork airport is five miles south of the centre. Two bus operators offer links to the city. A cab to the city centre costs €15–€20 (£12.50–£17).

Check in
MacCurtain Street has a range of accommodation – including the characterful three-star Hotel Isaacs at number 48. On the south side of town, Jurys is a stylish 21st-century hotel off Western Road. There are also plenty of B&Bs along Western Road. Cork has several backpacker hostels, of which the most attractive is Kinlay House on Bob & Joan's Walk.

Take a hike
Start at the National Monument just opposite the tourist office. Walk north, away from the river, along the handsome Grand Parade, which was once a waterway. Turn right into St Patrick's Street. Look to the left to see the Huguenot Quarter. Many Protestants from France came here in the 17th century, and it is now full of bars, restaurants and shops. At the north channel of the River Lee, turn right to follow Merchant's Quay, before walking south along Parnell Place. At the south channel, look across to the handsome City Hall.

Cultural afternoon
The Crawford Municipal Art Gallery on Emmet Place has been extended to show a wide range of Irish art. The Butter Museum in O'Connell Square explores butter's role in the development of Cork.

Window shopping
While St Patrick's Street is the main shopping area, Cornmarket Street is more interesting. It has the Coal Quay market and a new shopping mall, the Cornmarket Centre.

An aperitif
Most visitors are keen to find a traditional Irish pub. Happily, there are still many of these – such as Dennehy's on Cornmarket Street.

Dining with the locals
Gourmet vegetarian dishes are on the menu at Café Paradiso, at 16 Lancaster Quay. Scoozi's, at 314 Winthrop Avenue, is cheaper, meatier and more relaxed, and offers alfresco dining in summer.

Take a ride
Bus 224 departs from Merchant's Quay, taking 20 minutes to reach Blarney, which is five miles north-west. Blarney Castle is a 15th-century fortress residence in landscaped grounds. The climb to the tower is narrow and difficult, but the views are spectacular.

Interesting? Click here to explore further.

1 Before you watch, think about this quesion: which do you prefer, the city or the countryside?

2 Watch the video. Who talks about these things? Write J (Joanna) or L (Luis).

1 the place where he/she lives   _____

2 a place where he/she goes on holiday   _____

3 According to Joanna, are the sentences true or false? Watch again (00:11–00:59) to check.

1 Gdansk is a city on the north coast of Poland.	TRUE / FALSE
2 Gdansk is a very long way from Sweden.	TRUE / FALSE
3 The north part of Sweden is very natural and wild.	TRUE / FALSE

4 According to Luis, are the sentences true or false? Watch again (01:05–01:45) to check.

1 Coffee is Colombia's biggest industry.	TRUE / FALSE
2 Colombia has a lot of natural resources.	TRUE / FALSE
3 Many Colombians have moved away from the cities.	TRUE / FALSE

5 Watch again (00:11–00:59) and try to complete what Joanna says using the adjectives in the box.

appealing   intriguing   mysterious   unspoilt

I particularly like its northern part, which is known as Europe's last wilderness, which means one of the few places that are ^{1}_____ and very ^{2}_____ . It will probably sound a little bit selfish, but I'm concerned that as more and more people discover this place for their own, it will become less ^{3}_____ and therefore, to me, less ^{4}_____.

6 If you *spoil* something, you damage or destroy it. If something is a *mystery*, it is strange or difficult to understand. What do you think *unspoilt*, *mysterious* countryside is like?

7 Circle the correct meaning for these words.

1 *Intriguing* means fascinating / boring.

2 *Appealing* means large / attractive.

8 Complete the information about Colombia using the words in the box. Watch Luis again (01:05–01:45) to check.

clothing   coal   coffee   financial   oil   printing

COLOMBIA

Natural resources: ^{1}___coal___ , ^{2}_____

Agriculture: ^{3}_____

Business: ^{4}_____ services

Manufacturing: ^{5}_____ , ^{6}_____

9 Do you prefer to spend your free time in a very quiet place, or somewhere with a lot to see and do?

GLOSSARY

drawn to (verb): If you are **drawn to** something, you like it and find it interesting.

wilderness /ˈwɪldənəs/ (noun): a very wild area of land, with no buildings or agriculture

selfish (adjective): When you are **selfish**, you think about you, not about other people.

discover (verb): to find or learn about something

therefore (conjunction): so, as a result

coal (noun): a hard black mineral which you burn for heat

printing (noun): the production of newspapers, books, etc.

manufacturing (noun): making things in an industrial way

Unit 1

1 b calypso c salsa d hip-hop e reggae f classical music
   g folk music

2 2 brought up; play 3 traditional 4 how 5 to

3 2 e 3 g 4 f 5 c

4 2 have a look 3 Hang on 4 think about 5 not really into
   6 that looks 7 sounds 8 see if 9 idea

5 2 skiing 3 yoga 4 volleyball 5 hockey 6 karate
   7 aerobics 8 swimming

6 1 karate 2 skiing 3 boxing

7 1 In heavy industrial sites and petro-chemical plants.
   2 He's a singer.

8 Songs from the 1940s and '50s (and musicals).

9 2 Did; have 3 did; decide 4 does; sing
   5 does; sing 6 Does; sing 7 is; doing

10 1 (He learned) by watching the films they were in again and again.
   2 No, he had a terrible voice.
   3 Because he wanted to join a musical group.
   4 (He sings) in musicals.
   5 (He usually sings) with the local (music) group.
   6 Yes, he does.
   7 He's preparing a part for the musical *Hello, Dolly!*.

11 1 True. Two teams of six players try to push a heavy circular
      'puck' into a goal at the bottom of a swimming pool.
   2 True. It's very popular in New Zealand, where it started.
   3 False. They throw plastic discs, like Frisbees.
   4 True. The players play chess for four minutes, then box for two
      minutes, for up to 11 rounds.
   5 True. Korfball is similar to basketball, and *korf* is the name for
      the basket.

13 b 6 c 5 d 1 e 4 f 3

14 2 False 3 True 4 False

15 2 b 3 a 4 a 5 a 6 b

DVD-ROM Extra

2 1 b 2 c 3 a

3 1 H, C 2 M, C

4 3, 5, 4, 1, 2

5 2 black 3 white 4 19/nineteen 5 19/nineteen 6 larger

6 1 T 2 T 3 F (He liked football and basketball.)
   4 F (He liked the people and the place.) 5 T

Unit 2

1 2 degree 3 exams 4 an exam 5 a degree 6 college
   7 an exam 8 studies

2 2 It's the most difficult subject I've / I have ever studied.
   3 I've / I have always enjoyed studying alone.
   4 I've / I have done a lot of exams in my life.
   5 I've / I have never written an essay in English.
   6 I've / I have done several part-time courses.
   7 She's the best teacher I've / I have ever had.
   8 I've / I have never failed an exam.

3 2 holiday 3 pay 4 stressful 5 place 6 flexible
   7 atmosphere 8 management 9 easy
   10 part-time 11 at home

4 2 've/have known; since
   3 's/has been; for
   4 's/has worked; for
   5 've/have lived; since
   6 've/have liked; since
   7 's/has played; since
   8 's/has been; for

5 2 in 3 in 4 in 5 in 6 – 7 at 8 to

6 1 False 2 False 3 False

8 1 True 2 False

9 2 I would like
   3 advertised
   4 I have worked
   5 I have studied
   6 I enjoy
   7 I have difficulty in
   8 improve my spoken English
   9 project the company's image effectively
   10 Regards

DVD-ROM Extra

2 1 b 2 c

3 1 c 2 e 3 a 4 b 5 d

4 1 T 2 F (There was space for about 20 people.)
   3 F (They didn't need a partner.) 4 T 5 T

5 2 back 3 really 4 so much 5 people

Unit 3

1 empty, friendly, convenient, expensive, noisy

2 2 modern/old-fashioned 3 cheap/expensive
   4 inconvenient/convenient 5 quiet/noisy 6 crowded/empty

3 2 noisy 3 friendly 4 cheap 5 convenient

4 Waiter: 1, 2, 3, 5, 9, 11
   Customer: 4, 6, 7, 8, 10, 12

5 2 No problem, come this way, please.
   3 Are you ready to order?
   4 And for you?
   5 Me too, please – soup.
   6 Anything to drink?
   7 Could we have a bottle of water, please?
   8 Sparkling or still?
   9 Can we have the bill, please?

6 2 bottle of red wine 3 table in the corner
   4 chicken in garlic sauce 5 meal for 25 people
   6 menu with lots of vegetarian dishes

7 2 What about 3 How about 4 What about 5 How about
   6 What should

9 2 chicken 3 mushrooms 4 prawns 5 pear 6 soup
   7 pasta 8 cheese 9 strawberries 10 potatoes

10 1 b 2 c 3 a 4 d

11 1 c 2 b 3 d 4 a

12 Pete: Bella Napoli
    Ravi: El Buho Azul
    Sonia: The Taj

DVD-ROM Extra

2 almonds, anchovies, chicken, chilli, coconut rice, ginger,
   monkey nuts, onions, pistachios, spring onions

3 1 lokum 2 nasi lemak 3 nasi lemak 4 lokum

4 1 had 2 became 3 opened

5 1 is 2 come 3 cook

6 Nilgun uses the past simple because she is relating facts from
   the past.
   Alex uses the present simple because he is describing facts that
   are still true.

Unit 4

1 2 passengers 3 meter 4 fare 5 change 6 tip 7 receipt

2 2 T 3 P 4 T 5 P 6 P 7 T 8 P

3 1 How much is it to the airport?
   2 Can I put my bags in the back?
   3 Can you take me to Terminal 2, please?
   4 That's $27.80, please.
   5 can I have a receipt, please?
   6 Have a good trip, then.

4 2 After 3 then 4 During 5 When

5 2 paid 3 realised 4 was crying 5 saw 6 gave

6 2 to 3 in 4 in/to 5 – 6 for 7 with 8 for 9 to 10 in/–
7 b 4 c 2 d 5 e 1
8 1 b 2 c 3 a
9 2 because 3 to 4 for 5 because 6 because 7 for 8 to
11 b
12 a 4 b 3 c 1 d 2

DVD-ROM Extra

1 2 French 3 Japanese 4 Japanese 5 Afghanistan 6 India
3 1 Switzerland 2 Swiss; Japanese 3 Afghan
   4 English; French 5 English; French 6 India; Afghanistan
   7 Hindi
4 1 magnificent; beautiful 2 nice 3 unusual 4 little
   5 beautiful
5 2 family 3 different 4 actually 5 lifestyle

Unit 5

1 A 4 B 2 C 3
2 3 Sorry, do you have any smaller notes?
   1 Hello. Can I change these euros into Canadian dollars, please?
   4 Sure. Are twenties OK?
   2 Of course. That's 50, 100, 150, 200 euros. So that's $332.22.
     Here you are.
   5 Fine. Thanks.
3 2 pay 3 cards 4 PIN 5 receipt
4 1 How would you like to pay?
   2 how much is it?
   3 I'll pay in cash.
   4 Do you have anything smaller?
5 2 d 3 a 4 e 5 c
6 2 can 3 don't have to 4 should 5 Don't 6 shouldn't
   7 shouldn't 8 don't have to 9 shouldn't 10 You have to
7 Across: 4 currency 5 cash 6 coins 7 PIN 8 notes
   Down: 1 dollars 2 by 3 receipt 4 change
8 All of them
9 2 Bad 3 Bad 4 Good 5 Bad 6 Good 7 Bad 8 Good
10 2 b 3 a 4 a 5 b 6 b

DVD-ROM Extra

2 2 AL 3 AL 4 AL 5 AL 6 M 7 AL 8 M
3 1 F (She thinks credit cards are better.) 2 T 3 T 4 T
   5 F (She thinks it is a good use of technology.)
4 2 he's only learned 3 he's doing 4 he gets 5 picks up
5 1

Unit 6

1 2 Doing [the] cooking
   3 Doing [the] dusting
   4 doing [the] ironing
   5 Cleaning [the] windows
   6 Doing [the] vacuuming
2 1 b 2 c 3 c 4 a
4 2 f 3 c 4 e 5 b 6 d
5 2 Lightning 3 Tornado 4 Heavy rain 5 Hail 6 A rainbow
6 2 hotter 3 most important 4 further 5 beautiful
   6 most popular
7 2 cooler 3 cloudier 4 hottest 5 wettest
8 3 and 4
10 Example answers
   2 I don't **really** like football.
   3 **Could you** be quiet, **please? / Would you mind being** quiet,
     please? / Do you think you could be quiet, **please?**
   4 This **isn't very interesting.**
   5 **Could you tell me** the time, **please?**
12 2 in 3 at 4 for 5 on
13 Peter H

14

positive	negative
big	could have been better
comfortable	disappointing
friendly	far from the centre
great	not very clean
in a quiet area	rude
ready to help	too small
	uncomfortable
	unhelpful

15 2 could have been cleaner 3 would prefer 4 don't mind
   5 more expensive
16 2 a 3 d 4 b 5 e

DVD-ROM Extra

2 1 c 2 a 3 b
3 1 F (They stay at home more in winter.)
   2 F (They talk less in winter.) 3 T 4 T
   5 F (They left Rio in summer.) 6 T
4 1 quite; really; really; really; really
   2 quite
5 1 really 2 really 3 really 4 quite
6 It was **really** hot when they left Rio de Janeiro, but when they got
   to Tierra del Fuego, it was **really** cold. They didn't have the right
   clothes, but they wrapped up **really** warm with all the clothes they
   had. They stayed indoors **quite** a lot, but they did go out and see
   some penguins.

Unit 7

1 1 oil 2 flooding 3 polluted 4 traffic
   5 sea level 6 climate 7 transport
2 1 6 2 2,5 3 1,7 4 4
3 1 a 2 c 3 b
5 2 e 3 c 4 d 5 a 6 b
6 1 she has 2 you go; you'll see 3 I'll send; I find
   4 I have; I might call 5 you go; you should go
   6 you look; you'll see
7 The tourist office is b.
8 2 you'll see 3 Go along 4 turn 5 you continue 6 go past
   7 on your 8 you'll come
9 2 a map 3 a restaurant 4 leaflets 5 the bus station
   6 art galleries
10 2 Have you got
   3 do you have any information about
   4 Do you organise
   5 Do you sell
   6 can you recommend
11 Across: 7 station 8 square 9 tour 10 canal
   Down: 1 tourist office 2 gardens 4 museum 5 palace
   6 sights
12 2 e 3 g 4 h 5 c 6 f 7 d 8 i 9 a
13 2 False 3 False 4 True 5 True 6 False 7 False
14 people who like sightseeing and culture

DVD-ROM Extra

2 1 L 2 J
3 1 T 2 F (Gdansk is very close to Sweden.) 3 T
4 1 F (It's not the biggest business any more.) 2 T
   3 F (They have moved away from the countryside.)
5 1 unspoilt 2 mysterious 3 intriguing 4 appealing
6 wild, unpolluted, without buildings, and with quite a strange
   atmosphere
7 1 fascinating 2 attractive
8 2 oil 3 coffee 4 financial 5 printing 6 clothing